Ausome Parenting

The Guide to Endless Love,
Emotional Support, and Acceptance
for Your Autistic Child

Natalie Loveson

Copyright

<u>Disclaimer Notice:</u>

Professional and creative illustrator Katie Borkin deserves special credit for bringing this book to life with her theme illustrations.

First published: January 2024

ISBN: 978-965-93147-7-5 – paperback

ISBN: 978-965-93147-1-3 – eBook

For information contact: natalie@ausomeparentingbooks.com

Contents

Get your FREE gift!

Want to get the most out of this book? Start with 'Ausome Answers'. This quick read offers powerful insights from autistic adults, giving you a deeper understanding of your child's unique needs and how you can be their best advocate

Get a copy by visiting

https://bf.ausomeparentingbooks.com/gpjju3afsd

OR Scan this code with you mobile device:

Introduction

Children with autism are colorful—they are often very beautiful and, like the rainbow, they stand out.

Adele Devine

Let's face it—parenting, in general, can be an emotional rollercoaster thanks to the unexpected twists and turns when you least expect them. Those overwhelming moments leave you wondering whether you've even got this figured out or are simply winging it. The journey becomes even more colorful when autism is in the mix. With this diagnosis, you never know what's to come, as every child is different. But don't worry because, in this book, I will share some expert guidance, practical steps, and essential strategies to help you handle what's to come. I've been in your shoes, as my son, Idan, was diagnosed when he was two-and-a-half.

Now, he's six years old and thriving, yet I'm still learning more about him and autism every day. That being said, I aim to remind you to celebrate the moments of wonder that come as a perk of being a parent to an autistic child.

But fear not; I won't give you some cookie-cutter solutions that you could get with a simple Google search. I understand there is no one-size-fits-all concept when raising exceptional kids, especially when autism is added to your parenting plan. So, I will help you navigate this labyrinth through personal experiences, anecdotes, and strategies backed with scientific evidence. What makes me believe that I can do an effective job in the matter? Well, because I've been in your shoes, and I know that even though raising your kids the right way is important, you need to do it while preserving your own sanity.

My mother always used to tell me when I was a kid that life's greatest adventures often begin with a twist, and I never thought I would realize the truth behind this statement until I became the mother of an autistic child. I was a first-time mom, eagerly waiting to embrace parenthood, armed with so many dreams, milestones we wanted to meet, and an unending love for someone who wasn't even born. But life had something extraordinary planned for me, changing the course of my family's story forever.

Every time I recall the moment I heard my child's diagnosis, it brings back a storm of emotions for me. The room felt cold, and the sterile, white walls around me didn't help ease the feeling in my heart. I remember the doctor trying to explain what it meant. He was very gentle, of course, yet matter-of-fact at the same time, but all I could hear was the word "autism." All the connotations and uncertainty that came to mind with this single word hung in the air with so much heaviness that I simply couldn't breathe. Everything seemed blurry as I had tears welling up in my eyes and my husband holding me steady. I would not say that the tears were of guilt, something I may have done or didn't do to cause my child's autism. No, they were more from a feeling of overwhelm and a mixture of confusion and fear.

I could feel that I clutched onto two realities in that very moment—one was of the dreams I had woven of the life we could have had, and the other was the life that lay ahead of us. Even though I wasn't exactly aware of the details that lay ahead, I did know that the map of our lives was quickly redrawn with that single diagnosis and that many twists and turns were waiting along the path. But

I also developed a fierce determination as a mother to deal with everything that comes our way to give our child the best possible life. The way forward was indeed unknown and daunting for us, who knew nothing about autism other than the myths that society threw at us. Still, amidst those clouds of uncertainty, there was hope.

In the weeks that followed, I, along with my husband, started on a journey of discovery—and this showed me the resilience that we all had as a family as we came to know more about the colorful world of autism. It was then that I discovered an autism diagnosis comes with its own stages of acceptance.

I moved through the denial and disbelief, then the anger that my child would have to deal with this disorder for the rest of their life. From there, I went on to bargaining, thinking that I could magically change the diagnosis with enough positive thoughts and affirmations, or the doctor would call me back and tell me they had made a mistake. Then, I moved on to depression, which only made me feel worse because I couldn't help thinking about my child's future. *Would they be able to live a normal life? Make friends? Drive a car? Get a job? Live on their own?* These are the questions I worried about the most. However, once I remembered who my child was and how strong they were, I stepped out of my depression and moved on to the last stage: acceptance.

I started this book with a quote from Adele Devine because, as a mother of an autistic child, I have come to realize through my journey that these extraordinary children have vibrant hues just like the rainbow. Every child on the autistic spectrum is unique in their own way. It truly is this spectrum of colors that has changed my understanding, mindset, life, and purpose as a parent forever, and I'm so glad it did. I had some of the most challenging and beautiful moments in my life after that diagnosis, but I've also celebrated every small victory ever since then, whether it was a precious hug or a simple word spoken, with unfettered joy. That's because each moment was a living testament to my child's progress.

I will also agree that it was not a bed of roses. The journey was not without its trials. But, as my husband says, with some patience, love, and a sprinkle of humor, we can conquer any mountain that stands in our way. Every morning, I see my child's endless curiosity, quirks, and, of course, the boundless amount of love they have in their heart. I know I am my child's biggest advocate in the world, and that will never change. With that in mind, I now not only celebrate the uniqueness that autistic kids have, but I have also learned and embraced neurodiversity.

I have an educational background in nursing and bioresearch, which, to some extent, provided me with a solid foundation when it came to child psychology. However, it was my child's spirit that fueled me to keep digging deeper. This journey gifted me a wealth of wisdom while, at the same time, challenging my assumptions and transforming my perspective. To be completely honest, it was a path of continuous learning. I realized that if you truly want to understand the autistic spectrum, it goes beyond academic knowledge because a certain part is also about connecting with these kids on their level.

I want to thank each and every one of you for deciding to join me on this adventure. I wanted to write this book so that I can provide fellow parents of children with autism with a comprehensive guide that will not only offer them expert guidance, but also some practical tips and strategies. My intention is to be your companion throughout the highs and lows and, most of all, to remind you that you are not alone.

Whether you're a parent who's completely new to the world of autism or seeking strategies that actually work, this book has valuable information for everyone. At the same time, I never wanted this book to come off as just another copy of the autism guide for parents you'll get on the market, but rather, to go beyond that. It's about seeing the world through the eyes of the autistic children themselves. This book will help you break down the barriers of communication and understand the complex emotions of your ki d.

Above everything else, I want to dedicate this book to empowering parents like you, who provide unwavering support, encouragement, and inspiration throughout the parenting journey. I know all too well that you need an unyielding spirit, a whole lot of resilience, and courage to be a parent to an autistic child in this cruel world, but throughout the pages of this book, I will provide you with reassurance in the form of anecdotes. I'm sure you'll find comfort in knowing that you are not the only one facing those challenges because I did, too, and so are countless other parents.

There will be days when the doubts creep in, leaving you feeling overwhelmed and emotionally drained. On those days, you must remind yourself that, with every step you take, you are bringing yourself closer to understanding your child's needs and the remarkable person they are becoming.

So, dear parents, are you ready to take that first step with me? As you turn the pages of this book, you will find that every chapter has new and valuable information that will deepen and enrich your connection with your child. If you want to create a world where there's no limit to acceptance or boundaries to love, let's begin this voyage together. I promise the journey is just as exciting and breathtaking as the destination.

CHAPTER 1

Uncovering the Truth About Autism

If you've met one person with autism, you've met one person with autism.

Dr. Stephen Shore

Despite the fact that the term "autism" was coined all the way back in 1911, there are so many misconceptions about the disorder over a century later. Whether Autism Spectrum Disorder (ASD) is represented in movies, TV shows, or social media, these platforms tend to forget to include some crucial information.

Sure, TV shows and movies highlight some well-known facts, like sensory issues or the incessant need for a structured routine, but the characters exhibiting these symptoms all tend to act the exact same way. They are painted as the weirdos, freaks, or outcasts of the entire school or within their workplace, sometimes even within their own family. Then, there's the fact that social media platforms like TikTok have made autism "a trend," essentially trivializing the condition and the people who have it. The worst part is that ASD is not a visible disorder, so it's difficult to call out those claiming to have it just so they can appear "cool" or "quirky."

The way autism is represented in the news and media is essentially hit or miss, meaning that while some shows, such as *Parenthood* and *Atypical*, have done a great job of depicting the impact the disorder has on those who have it and their families, some are spreading misinformation. So, that's why, in this chapter, we will introduce and discuss all the necessary questions to help you connect, understand, and discover the unexplored aspects of autism.

The purpose of this information, which has been thoroughly researched and collected by reputable resources that aren't TikTok, is to help you change the life of your child in a positive direction. Moreover, it will also highlight various fallacies surrounding autism and the person living with it, as these myths often hinder the proper development of an autistic individual, thereby influencing the normal life of the whole family.

Six Ws to Understand Autism Better

What Is Autism or Autism Spectrum Disorder?

According to Autism Speaks (2021), Autism Spectrum Disorder, also known as autism or ASD, is a condition characterized by challenges with repetitive behaviors, socialization, and communication, both verbal and nonverbal. Despite popular belief, the disorder is not a one-size-fits-all condition, but rather a spectrum that includes many subtypes and levels of severity. While one child may learn to talk at a very young age, they might struggle with other aspects, such as making friends or stimming (which we will discuss later) when upset, overwhelmed, or nervous.

What Is the Age at Which Autism Can Be Diagnosed in a Child?

Although the signs of ASD begin around the age of two or three in children and last their entire lives, many children may not receive an official diagnosis until they are much older. However, since the disorder can't be discovered using blood tests or brain scans, a child as young as 18 months old can be diagnosed by a trained medical professional after observing the child's behavior and development (CDC, 2022).

What Is Autism for a Growing Child?

As children with autism hit their preteen and teenage years, it's common for them to struggle with making friends, maintaining relationships, communicating with those around them, and understanding their role at school or work. They may also struggle with mental health disorders, such as depression, anxiety, and attention-deficit hyperactivity disorder (ADHD), as these conditions are more likely to occur in those with ASD than those without (CDC, 2022).

What Is it Like to Raise an Autistic Child?

Considering that autism can cause a delay in communication, sensory issues, emotional dysregulation, and difficulty with socialization, raising a child who is autistic can be overwhelming and stressful for parents. Some days are worse than others, like when the meltdowns seem to be never-ending, but there are many ways parents of children with autism can intervene and help make life easier for everyone. We will discuss the different types of intervention throughout the coming chapters.

Why Is Autism More Common in Boys as Compared to Girls?

Research states that boys are four times more likely to be autistic than girls (UofM, 2017). Although girls can clearly have the disorder, scientists believe that the Y chromosome, which you probably recall from your high school health class as the male chromosome, makes boys more susceptible and predisposed to ASD. Also, there's the fact that boys are more likely to be diagnosed with autism than girls because the latter is better at "masking" or mirroring the behaviors of neurotypical children to hide their symptoms.

When girls mask their symptoms, it's harder for doctors to narrow down a specific diagnosis, often leading the female to be misdiagnosed with other disorders such as ADHD or anxiety.

What do Statistics Reveal About Autism in Children?

While the children who have yet to be diagnosed or have been misdiagnosed with another condition aren't included, the Center for Disease Control and Prevention (CDC) estimated that 1 in 36 US children are on the autism spectrum. In 2020, there was a rise in autism diagnoses among eight-year-olds, with the CDC stating that 1 in 44 second graders had been diagnosed with the condition (Autism Speaks, 2023).

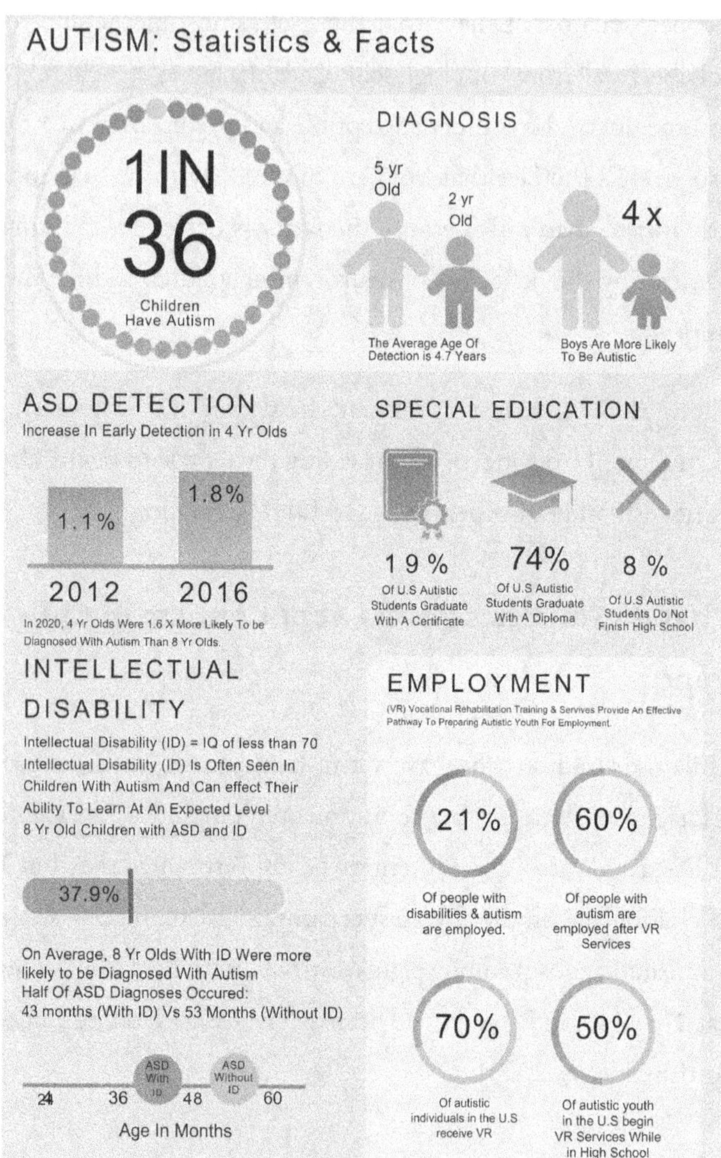

Source: AUTISM AND DEVELOPMENTAL DISABILITIES MONITORING (ADDM) NETWORK, n.d., 2023

Demystifying the Fallacies Associated With Autism

Autism Spectrum Disorder is a condition that many would consider to be misunderstood. The amount of myths regarding the disorder is overwhelming, making it difficult to know what's true and what's not. Luckily, I have compiled and dispelled the most common myths so you can be more aware of the facts before we dive into the specifics.

Autism Is an Illness

An illness refers to a disease that is contagious or otherwise makes you sick. Illnesses can also be cured with medication or other medical interventions. ASD, on the other hand, is a neurological disorder, and although the symptoms can get better with various therapeutic interventions, there isn't a cure.

People With Autism are Emotionless

This particular myth is extremely hurtful for those with autism. Just like any other human being, people with autism can and do feel emotions just like anyone else. The only difference is that they might express them differently. Remember, one of the hallmark signs of autism is the difficulty of communicating and socializing with others. With that being said, someone with autism also often struggles to read social cues. Combine all of these and you get someone who isn't sure how to communicate what they are feeling, if their reaction is appropriate, or if their emotions match those around them. This uncertainty can make them look disinterested or "emotionless," whereas they are simply trying to interpret their feelings.

On the other hand, sometimes big emotions can cause big reactions and be overwhelming, causing a person with autism to self-soothe using stimming or repetitive behaviors or with a meltdown if they become overstimulated.

Autism Hinders One's Independence

This myth couldn't be further from the truth. While some people with autism may require assistance, the disorder affects everyone differently. There are many children and adults with autism who are very independent, whether it's being self-sufficient, holding a job, cleaning up after themselves, or making a home-cooked meal. Even if someone is lacking in certain areas, they can always use occupational therapy to learn the skills they need to be independent. Like any child or teenager, it's possible to be independent if they have the right resources and support.

Autism is Diagnosed Only in Childhood

Interestingly, many adults have been diagnosed with autism due to the change in diagnostic criteria. Oftentimes, the person was misdiagnosed with a different condition at a younger age, such as depression, ADHD, or anxiety. In a recent study, Psychiatry professor Laurent Mottron examined the Danish National Patient Registry and discovered that 2,199 of Denmark's adult population was diagnosed with autism after age 18. Mottron concluded that the reason for the delay in diagnosis is the change in criteria from when the person was born until now (Hess, 2022). Also, there has been a major increase in parents who discovered they were autistic after their child was diagnosed, many of them stating that they didn't recognize their traits as a symptom until it was pointed out (Moorhead, 2021).

All Autistic People Exhibit the Same Symptoms

As stated earlier, autism is a spectrum, meaning that while some people with the disorder will experience severe symptoms, such as being non-verbal, having a lower IQ, and extreme sensitivities, others symptoms may be milder. The point is that no two people experience autism symptoms the same.

Autism Is Caused by Vaccines

After much speculation, the CDC has conducted many studies and plenty of research to dispel this myth. They have stated on multiple occasions that there is no evidence or proof of a link between ASD and vaccines. Rather, autism is a disorder caused by other risk factors, such as gender, environmental factors, and genetics (CDC, 2021).

Autism Makes One Violent

This myth is another that is considered hurtful and adds to the already over-stigmatized disorder. People with autism are no more violent than those without ASD. While it can co-occur with behavioral disorders, such as ADHD or oppositional defiant disorder (ODD), autism alone doesn't make them behave violently. Oftentimes, if a child with autism were to kick, hit, or bite others, it's usually because they are having difficulty expressing their feelings or needs and lash out due to frustration. However, these are issues that can be dealt with in therapy, not something they are doomed to live with for the rest of their lives.

Autistic People Cannot Lead a Normal Life

People with autism can most certainly live a normal life. In fact, there are doctors, lawyers, scientists, parents, teachers, and so many others who are living with an autism diagnosis and live a normal, independent life. They can have friends, have romantic relationships, pay their bills on time, drive, basically anything that a neurotypical person can do.

Conclusion

In this chapter, we explored the six Ws of autism. You learned what autism is, the average age of diagnosis, why boys are more likely than girls to have the disorder, some interesting statistics, and what it's like to raise a child with autism. We also demystified the most common fallacies about autism.

As you can see, autism isn't a one-size-fits-all type of disorder. It has many aspects, from the range of symptoms to how it affects the person. It also doesn't mean someone with autism is doomed to live with their parents forever, being waited on hand and foot. They have the ability to be independent, hold a job, make and maintain relationships, and so much more. It's also important to remember that while shows and movies, like *Good Doctor* and *Rainman*, try to represent those living with ASD, they are intended for entertainment purposes. Not everyone with autism is a savant, nor are they mentally disabled. In fact, only 1 in 10 people with autism show some form of savant skills (SSM Health, n.d.).

The point is, before you can help your child to thrive despite their autism diagnosis, you have to know what the disorder entails. To do so, you have to separate fact from fiction. However, now that you know that the vaccine your child received didn't cause their disorder or that, given the right resources and support, they can still become a functioning member of society, we can dive into the next chapter where we explore the risk factors, early signs and symptoms, and the red flags of autism.

Screening Your Child for Autism

The most interesting people you'll find are ones that don't fit into your average cardboard box. They'll make what they need, they'll make their own boxes.

Dr. Temple Grandin

When you first realize your child is somewhat different from other children their age, it's normal to be a little scared. You think back on your entire pregnancy and their age to this point, wondering if something you did or didn't do could have changed the wiring of their brain. However, as you read in Chapter 1, this isn't the case.

Nothing you did or neglected to do causes autism, but that doesn't mean that you shouldn't consider having your child screened for the disorder.

This chapter will examine the major risk factors associated with autism. We will also shed light on the early visible symptoms that act as warning signs and indicate that the actions and behaviors your child is exhibiting might be autism. But before we begin, I want you to know that I am aware of how scary the screening phase can be. I've been where you are and know all too well how nerve-wracking it can be to look at your child, who is absolutely perfect in your eyes, and wonder what's wrong with them. Just know that you are not alone and a lot of parents have been through this stage. You will make it through; it just takes time, effort, patience, and the support of the people you love.

Risk Factors of Autism

While researchers have yet to find the definitive cause of ASD, a large number agree that the disorder is one a child is born with (Elkins & Sharon, 2014). Essentially, your child came into this world autistic, so nothing you do now or did in the past will change that. However, it's always good to know the risk factors behind autism.

- **Premature or low birth weight:** Children born before 30 weeks have a high likelihood of being autistic. Also, researchers have discovered that children who have a very low birth weight are five times more likely to be diagnosed with some form of ASD (Hatch, 2011).

- **Having autistic siblings:** Genetics also play a major factor in the likelihood of your child having autism. If one of your children has already been diagnosed, there's a much higher chance of your other children having the disorder as well. Similarly, your child also has an increased chance of having ASD if either a parent or close relative has it.

- **Child's gender:** As you learned in the previous chapter, boys are four times more likely to be diagnosed with autism than girls.

- **Parents' age:** Although more research is needed, researchers have found a link between children with autism and having parents of advanced age (Hatch, 2011). This means that children whose parents are over the age of 40 when they were born are more likely to have autism spectrum disorder.

- **Other medical conditions:** Certain disorders increase the likelihood of an autism diagnosis. These conditions include Rett syndrome, tuberous sclerosis, and fragile X syndrome.

You might notice as you read through these risk factors that race, ethnicity, religion, or economic status aren't included. Why? Because these four things don't increase your child's chances of having autism. Any child of any race or ethnicity can be autistic; the disorder does not discriminate. You could be the richest person in the world, and your child could still have autism.

Early Signs and Symptoms in Young Children

As I mentioned earlier, a child can be diagnosed with autism as early as 18 months old, although this isn't common. Some signs and symptoms may indicate your son or daughter's doctor should keep a close eye on their progress and age-appropriate milestones. As you may know, milestones are developmental markers each child reaches at a certain age. When a child doesn't meet these markers consistently or reach many of them within a reasonable time, your child's pediatrician might become suspicious of a neurological disorder to blame.

Here are some of the signs and symptoms of autism in children under the age of one that you should look out for (*Signs of Autism in Babies and Toddlers*, n.d.; Gendel, 2022):

- **Rarely smiles or doesn't smile at all:** The milestone for smiling should be reached around six months. If your child isn't smiling before or around that time or imitating you when you smile at them, I would bring it up during your child's next wellness appointment. The doctor may want to check their vision first to ensure they are able to see your smile and rule out other causes.

- **Doesn't make eye contact:** Lack of eye contact is known as one of the major indicators that a child may have autism. Seeing as eye contact is a way to communicate with others and comprehend what's being said, the lack of eye contact may cause a child to struggle further down the line.

- **Struggles to follow objects with their eyes:** Similar to making eye contact, the inability or showing difficulty when following objects with their eyes is an indicator of ASD. Once again, it's not a surefire way of receiving an autism diagnosis, as your child's pediatrician may want to check their vision first to rule out any visual disruptions.

- **Doesn't respond when their name is called:** If your child reaches the age of 6–12 months old and doesn't respond to their name, you might be worried that they could be suffering from hearing loss. However, being unresponsive to one's name by this age is actually a sign of autism. If you notice this symptom, bring it up with your child's doctor, who will probably test your child's hearing to rule out hearing loss.

- **Limited or no reaction to loud sounds:** Most babies that aren't on the autism spectrum will search for the source of loud noises, whereas children with ASD might not care to find the source or even be startled. This might worry parents, especially if their baby's hearing has already been tested and appears to be fine any other time.

- **Repetitive body movements:** Frequently repeating certain movements, such as stiffening their limbs, flapping their hands, and standing or sitting in strange positions, are known as self-stimulatory behaviors or stimming. We will go over these behaviors in greater detail later on, but you should know that these repetitive gestures are often used to calm the person down when they feel overwhelmed or upset. They are also an indicator of autism.

- **Limited imitation of words or sounds:** Babies normally start to talk around the age of one, but they begin to imitate sounds or coo around the age of four months. They use the sounds and babbles to communicate with their loved ones, but if you notice a delay, it may be a sign of autism.

- **Displays an unusual dislike of physical affection:** Babies who show a disinterest in hugs, cuddles, and being picked up, or don't try to get their parent's attention to receive these things may have ASD. This dislike or disinterest may worsen as they get older, making it harder for them to bond with others.

- **Delay in motor development:** One of the biggest signs that your child may be on the spectrum is a delay in their motor skills. If they fail to reach milestones for crawling, rolling over, standing up, and feeding themselves with a spoon, your child's doctor might request further tests or an in-depth observation of the child's behaviors.

JUMPS IF EXCITED: *FLAPS* HANDS LIKE WINGS	REPEATS *YOUR* *QUESTIONS* INSTEAD OF ANSWERING *(ECHOLALIA)*	AVOIDS EYE CONTACT OR, CONVERSELY *STARES* EXCESSIVELY	DOESN'T ENGAGE *IN* PRETEND PLAY	DOESN'T *IDENTIFY* MOM OR DAD
CONSERVATIVE ABOUT SAME WALKING *ROUTES*	DOESN'T *RESPOND* WHEN *THEIR* NAME IS CALLED	DOESN'T ENJOY CLAPPING & FINGER GAMES	DOESN'T USE THE *POINTING* GESTURE	DOESN'T FOLLOW VERBAL INSTRUCTIONS
EATS *SELECTIVE* FOOD ONLY	DOESN'T USE MORE/STOP GIVE, GESTURES	**DOESN'T SPEAK**	USES YOUR HAND AS A TOOL	ENGAGES IMPROPER TOY PLAY
DOESN'T EXPRESS *YES* OR *NO* IN WORDS/ GESTURES	SENSITIVE TO *SOME* CLOTHES/ TEXTURES OR LABELS	DOESN'T SHOW INTEREST *IN* CHILDREN *THEIR* AGE	DOESN'T SHARE ATTENTION IN OBJECTS YOU *ARE* LOOKING AT	DOESN'T UNDERSTAND *YOUR* MESSAGE ENTIRELY OR PARTIALLY
EXHIBITS *REPETITIVE* BEHAVIOR DURING PLAYTIME	UNUSUAL *OVER* ATTACHMENT ON **TOYS/** OBJECTS	*REPEATS* SENTENCES FROM **CARTOONS** RANDOMLY	DOESN'T *INITIATE* COMMUNICATION	BUILDS *OBJECTS* IN ROWS

If Your Child Is Between 1.5 - 3 Years Old, And You Suspect They Might Be Different, Play This Bingo Game To Find 3 - 5 Common Signs Of Autism. I Hope You Lose This Bingo, But If You Win, Keep Reading!

As children get older and reach the two-year mark, there are other symptoms your child's doctor may notice or keep an eye on, especially if they suspect the child may have ASD. Here are the early signs and symptoms of autism in children between the ages of one and two years old (Paulos, 2018; *Signs of Autism in Babies and Toddlers*, n.d.):

- **Limited speech or makes sounds to communicate:** Toddlers on the spectrum may struggle to communicate their needs with others. While some may become non-verbal, other children may express themselves verbally through a language they created. A friend of mine had a two-year-old daughter who would communicate through sounds similar to what a guinea pig would make, ultimately leading her mother to have her evaluated and receive an autism diagnosis. Or, if the child does speak, their tone may always sound flat or unemotional.

- **Walks on their toes:** Toddlers with autism may walk on their toes for many reasons. Some might do it because that's how they learned how to walk and the rigidness in their behavior makes them want to keep walking that way. Their sensitivity to certain stimuli might make walking on their toes more soothing for them. They may also walk on their toes when they feel anxious or stressed, as many people experience a tightness in their muscles when they are dealing with a stressful situation. Alternatively, Stephen M. Edelson of the Autism Research Institute (2019) suggests that toe walking could be due to a dysfunctional vestibular system or neurological immaturity.

- **Inability to follow verbal instructions:** Toddlers on the autism spectrum often struggle to follow directions, regardless of how simple they are. The reason is that it often takes them longer to process what they are hearing and putting into action. There could also be a number of other reasons, such as the person giving the instructions talking too fast, the directions including more than one step, the environment around them being too loud for them to focus, or the steps aren't as simple as the speaker believes them to be.

- **Shows hyper fixation on certain topics or toys and disregards everything else:** Children with ASD often show a strong interest in one particular topic, such as dinosaurs, trains, or a specific type of toy. The same goes for toddlers. They might only want to show or talk to you about their interest and walk away if you try to talk or show them something other than that particular subject.

- **Unusual attachment to a particular toy or object:** Although most children grow out of having a favorite toy or blanket, toddlers with autism might prolong their enjoyment and continue to bring it everywhere they go. It might not even be a toy they prefer to carry around; it could be a household object, such as a certain blue

Teflon spatula. Sometimes, they might have a particular favorite toy and collect different versions of it. A friend of mine's child was obsessed with her Minnie Mouse stuffed animal, but didn't have a preference as to which one she took everywhere with her as she had at least 20 of them, each one a different color and wearing different clothes.

Another example is my child was obsessed and fixated on air-conditioned engines for almost three years, which started when he began to walk by himself at the age of two. He used to walk down the street for hours and never got tired, all because he wanted to see the engines on the buildings. He could watch them for 10–15 minutes each without moving, and every piece hypnotized him. He was amazed with the power of rotation of the wheel inside it and the big engines drew his attention. Nothing else distracted him or pulled his attention away to focus on other similar objects—small windmills, YouTube videos about windmills, or small ventilators. Lucky for us, he had lost his interest almost entirely by the time he was almost six.

- **Struggles to transition between activities:** A toddler who shows rigidness in their daily schedule might be on the autism spectrum. They might throw a fit or have a full-blown meltdown if there is a sudden change of plans or if something unexpectedly throws off their daily schedule. This rigidity may also translate over to other behaviors, such as only eating certain foods or refusing to eat or touch things with specific textures.

- **Repetitive behaviors during playtime:** This might include lining toys up from biggest to smallest or organizing them by color. Children on the spectrum may also show disinterest in pretend play, such as playing house, doctor, or pretending to be someone else. They may also find it more enjoyable to play with household objects rather than their toys, such as repeatedly opening and closing the refrigerator or cabinet doors.

- **Shows disinterest in playing with other children:** Many toddlers on the spectrum have no issue playing alone. In fact, they almost seem content or prefer to be on their own rather than finding children their age to play with. They might also withdraw from what's happening around them and seem to live in their own world.

There are many other symptoms that a young child might exhibit if they are on the autism spectrum, but remember that not all children show the same symptoms. They might not display all of these signs or they might exhibit all of them and more to different degrees. The signs and symptoms listed above are most commonly seen and noted during research studies or by doctors.

As your child grows out of the terrible twos, there are some "red flags" you should keep an eye out for. In this context I want to express my appreciation for a significant collaboration that greatly improved my understanding and influenced this section of the book. While researching and gathering information on raising a child with autism I had the privilege of working with Marina Fernsby, a friend and fellow advocate. Together we diligently documented warning signs that parents should know about.

The signs I write below are not meant to scare or overwhelm you, but to empower you with knowledge so that you can provide your child with the possible support. Let's explore these indicators further.

- **Lack of shared attention:** A neurotypical (or normally developing) child should be interested in what is currently interesting to an adult. During playtime with a child, shift your enthusiastic gaze to an object or toy and ask another adult to assess the child's behavior beforehand. Did the child catch your gaze, notice that you are interested in something, or shift their gaze to the object? Or did they continue with their own activities?

- **Participation in surrounding reality:** The child should be in the moment with you right now, be "here." If a suitcase falls with a bang somewhere nearby, do they look toward the source of the noise and then back at you to make sure you heard it as well? They should show with their actions and behavior that they understand what's happening around them.

For example, we were once at our friend's home, and they had a child the same age as mine. My son told me that he had lost his toy car somewhere. My friend's son jumped up and brought his car to him, even though no one asked him to do so. I'm not saying that your child should carry out long, drawn-out assignments, but they just need to "be with you." When a friend told me that her one-and-a-half-year-old child brought her shoes when they were going for a walk, I honestly thought she was lying and that this couldn't happen. My son allowed himself to be dressed and seated in the stroller but was a bored spectator in life, not an actor.

- **Seeking approval:** With this very look, a normal child asks for your reaction. Put the puzzle piece in the right place, then look at Mom. Put another one down, and again wait for Mom's reaction. They constantly want to tell you, "Look what I can do!" I have a video of my son at 3 ½-years-old where he spends 10 minutes picking out solar system planets cards and naming them from memory. He identified almost all of them, but didn't glance at me once; he simply didn't need or want my approval.

- **The child doesn't share joy:** A normal child will definitely bring Mom a toy car they found in the sandbox or a flower from the lawn. They will bring it and show it in an effort to share their joy. If you visit friends, your child will rummage through their toy boxes and constantly turn to you, showing what treasures they found inside. A child with autism doesn't feel the need to share their joy with you; they would much rather play alone.

- **Special abilities and interests:** Children with autism don't necessarily lag behind in mental development; on the contrary, they very often seem to teach themselves the alphabet, numbers, and colors. This is confusing, especially when you find yourself thinking that such a clever child simply can't have problems. Of course, this does not mean that all developed children should visit a psychiatrist; I just want to note that intelligence is not an excluding sign for autism. But, if a child has learned to read before learning to speak, this is hyperlexia—a direct signal to seek help. In American psychiatry, this is a "red flag" for autism.

- **Doesn't pay attention to people:** When a neurotypical child enters a new room or finds themselves in a new situation, they will look at the faces of the people present, even if they are shy and cling to their mom. A child with autism will glance over their faces or even not pay attention to them at all and will immediately go to the toys, doors, and other objects.

- **Improper toy play:** Even after multiple explanations of how to play properly, a child with autism may play with toys according to their own scenario. For example, they might take a ball and a pin and monotonously hit them against each other, bang a toy car on the garage door, endlessly open the doors of a toy house, and throw puzzle pieces inside. If you try to interrupt or distract them, a tantrum may occur.

Another sign of autism in infants and babies includes a disinterest in games most babies find enjoyable, like peek-a-boo. They may also struggle to imitate social cues, such as laughing or making facial expressions.

- **Routes:** A child with autism may want to walk only certain routes, and if you need to go somewhere else today, a tantrum may occur. My child, for example, until age four, refused to turn back (even if we forgot something and had to return). We would have to loop around some buildings and return to where we had previously been. Also, he would only walk on one side of the street; if we ended up on the other and he realized it, an uncontrollable tantrum began.

- **Fears:** Often, children with autism are terrified of strange things to the point of tantrums. My child was afraid of the washing machine during the spinning cycle or working dust vacuum. Later, he became afraid of pigeons sitting on the roof of our balcony. The noise they made was too scary to him and we always kept the door to the balcony closed and made the TV sound loud so he could not hear that noise. But if a child has only fears and nothing else from the list, it is most likely a separate problem.

- **Using mom's hand as a tool:** This is a very bright signal. A child with normal communication has many ways to get what they want from an adult. For example, my niece, who is neurotypical, poked her finger at me, then at a bottle of water, meaning "you, give water," when she was nine months old. An autistic child will grab the mom (or another person) by the hand and throw the hand toward the desired item—a toy on a shelf, a closed cabinet, and so on.

Children often use non-verbal cues such as waving, pointing, or grasping for items they want around 9–10 months of age. It's a way to communicate their wants and needs with their caregivers, so a limited use of these gestures might signal other issues.

- **Contact with parents:** In American diagnostics, the question of how a child *doesn't* communicate with primary caregivers, not with parents/guardians, is especially highlighted—because the contact with them can be wonderful! I didn't understand autism until my son, Idan, was three years old because he didn't go to kindergarten before then. I hadn't seen him interact with other people or children, but he interacted perfectly with me—enthusiastically responding to all my ideas for developmental activities, learning languages and numbers with me, and bringing me what he wanted to do. I didn't have a clue that something was wrong in our interaction. If you have contact with the child, but there are at least 5–10 signs from the above, it's very alarming.

- **Questions:** An autistic person probably doesn't ask them—none. Not to mention the questions regarding "why" things happened a certain way or "how" something worked. Everything they need, they already know; the rest does not bother them. Between the ages of 1 and 10, a neurotypical child asks questions, but with Idan, it was literally like living in the real-life version of the game "20 Questions." One time, when he was four years old, a boiler exploded outside the window of the neighboring house and began to splash water in every direction. He panicked and screamed, "What is it?! What is it?! What is this?!" That was his first question.

- **Raising hands to meet:** At about 10 months, a normal child, when parents are going to pick them up, will stretch their hands up to meet and lean toward their mom or dad. A child with autism allows himself to be picked up, but does not reach out.

- **Photography:** With a high probability, a child with autism older than two will not want to be photographed. If, in early childhood, you can still attract their gaze to the lens, but as they get older, it becomes more difficult. In almost all photos, they will look to the side, not into the frame.

- **Fairy tales:** A child with autism may look at picture books or encyclopedias, but they will not want to listen to fairy tales where someone said and did something. All these social nuances are absolutely uninteresting to them.

- **Controlling behavior:** A child with autism often instructs others on how to act, such as telling them where to sit, taking books to "read" to themselves, or forcing them to turn off music or the TV. Usually, adults laugh at this, saying, "Oh, a little boss," but this is one aspect of obsessiveness. Idan, for example, until the age of five, had to do everything first—put on his shoes first, leave the house first, walk down the road first; if someone overtook him or, God forbid, another child put on their shoes first in kindergarten, there would be a tantrum.

- **Empathy:** For typical children, some empathy is already evident by 18 months to two years of age. If they see a crying character on TV, they may try to wipe away their tears. However, if the mother of a child with autism cries out, "Oh, it hurts!" in front of them, the child will most likely ignore her or start crying out of irritation. A neurotypical child will, in each case, run to comfort their mother.

- **"Convenient" child:** Very often, children with high-functioning autism are seen as very "convenient" and trouble-free. They can occupy themselves for hours, do not require their mother's attention, and don't need to be entertained. I could put Idan on the carpet and lie down for a nap. When I woke up, I found him in the same place, engrossed in playing with toys. This is undoubtedly just one of the behavioral models, but it's worrisome if your child doesn't need anything from you.

- **Lack of initiative:** A child with autism may bring an item to their mother to meet their needs—to open a can of juice, unzip their bag, that is, or do anything they can't do themselves. But most likely, they will never initiate communication themselves. They won't approach you without reason, bring a toy and invite you to play, or show you a book they want you to read. They do not see the value in communication, often seeing their parents as service staff. At the same time, if the parents initiate the act of communication, they can accept it and participate (agree to your game, help you make snacks, tell you what movie they would like to watch, and so on).

- **Repetitive pattern in behavior:** This red flag can be pretty obvious. Repetitive behaviors include unusual bodily movements, such as flapping hands, flicking fingers, spinning around, or rocking back and forth. It could also include sounds, such as screaming, clearing their throat, or repeating words they hear.

- **Regression in developmental skills:** This might be one of the most worrisome red flags regarding autism. You beamed with pride when your child said their first word, took their first steps, and, really, anything they did for the first time. Then, suddenly, it's like everything changed. Everything they learned seems to have been deleted from their memory and they no longer talk, count, or know their colors. This is a common occurrence in some children on the autism spectrum. A friend of mine's son was speaking well before the age of one, but right after his second birthday, he just stopped. Not long after, he was diagnosed with autism.

- **Aggressive reactions:** If your child struggles to use words to express their emotions and instead lashes out aggressively, autism might be the reason behind their actions. These reactions include biting, smacking, kicking, and hitting others. They might also turn the aggression toward themself by hitting themselves, biting their hands or arms, or smacking their head on the ground. As you can imagine, acting out this way can be dangerous for them and others around them and should be brought to your child's doctor's attention immediately.

Also, although your child might not react to loud sounds, especially if they're the ones causing them, they might overreact to other stimuli. This could include high-pitched noises, bright lights, temperatures, or certain fabrics.

- **Hypersensitivity:** When a child with autism is sensitive to stimuli and sensory information around them, it's commonly known as hypersensitivity. If they don't like a certain sound, texture, fabric, or light brightness, they will do their best to avoid the stimuli as it causes extreme discomfort. Some children might even refuse to have their hair brushed or cut, brush their teeth with certain flavored toothpastes, and avoid certain smells. Hypersensitivity can also extend to their pain tolerance. Oversensitive children might act like they lost a limb when they get a paper cut.

What to Do if You Recognize These Signs and Symptoms in Your Child

When the suspicions arise in your brain, questioning whether your child could be one of the 36 children diagnosed with autism each year, it can be scary. Your mind wanders over the past few years, kicking yourself for missing the signs if they are, in fact, on the autism spectrum. You keep a close eye on them, thinking that maybe there's a reasonable explanation for the never-ending tantrums, incessant need to follow the daily routine, fight over brushing their hair every morning, and why they refuse to eat red meat.

You stand there, staring at them, thinking, *If I missed all the signs, I must be a terrible parent.* Well, I have news for you—you are an amazing parent. The fact that you are worried about your child and how their development is progressing is proof of that. Remember, the early signs and symptoms of autism start to show at different ages, and sometimes, the usual behaviors parents notice are just a phase as all children develop and learn new skills at their own pace. Some kids truly are "late bloomers," and the reason has nothing to do with autism. So, do yourself a favor and cut yourself some slack. What's important is that you are aware of the possibility now and willing to do something about it so your child can thrive.

So, if you notice any of the symptoms and signs listed in the section above, here are your next steps (Zuckerman, 2020):

1. **Spend lots of time with your child and observe their behaviors:** Pay close attention to how they play with you and by themselves. Make a mental note of repetitive behaviors, hyper-fixations, and if they are sensitive to certain stimuli. The more you focus on these signs, the more information you can give your child's doctor.

2. **Observe your child's behavior from afar as well:** Sometimes, children act in certain ways when they don't think anyone is paying attention. For example, they might feel more comfortable walking on their toes or flapping their hands if they think you aren't watching them. Children always try to imitate their parent's behaviors, so they might believe that their actions or behaviors are strange or unacceptable and try not to do them in front of others—even if it causes them to feel extremely anxious or

uncomfortable.

3. **Ask others if they have noticed any other signs or symptoms during the time they spent with your child:** There are many occasions when an outsider's perspective can be very helpful, and this is one of those times. Not only will getting input from your child's teacher, babysitter, or others who spend a considerable amount of time with your kid confirm the symptoms you have noticed, but they might also be able to tell you some behaviors they have personally seen.

4. **Compile your observations and write them down:** Although the next step is to take your concerns to your child's pediatrician, you should definitely consider writing down what you have observed as well as others' input. This is because when you are worried about your child and their development, you might not be thinking very clearly on the day of their appointment. All you want is answers, which might make it hard to keep all the details in your head. By taking the time to sit down and think, you can focus on everything you need to discuss with their doctor and ensure that you don't forget anything.

5. **Discuss your concerns with your child's doctor:** Your son or daughter might have a wellness check-up appointment soon; this would be the perfect time to bring up your concerns regarding your child's development. If they

don't have an appointment, you can call and make one at any time. Remember, early intervention is your best bet for a disorder like autism, so don't feel bad for requesting the soonest appointment available. You are your child's biggest advocate, so never feel guilty for putting their best interest first and getting a little pushy at times; just make sure you are being respectful about it.

6. **The day of the appointment:** Once you discuss your concerns with the pediatrician, don't be surprised if they make a series of follow-up appointments. They might want to observe your child's behaviors over the next few months before moving forward in case other issues are at play besides ASD.

Once they rule out other conditions, the pediatrician might refer to any number of specialists, including a neurologist, speech therapist, behavioral psychologist, or occupational therapist. Unlike the other three specialists listed, a neurologist can't make an official autism diagnosis; however, they can confirm that it's something to look into and observe your child's behavior so as to rule out other medical or neurological conditions.

These steps might sound overwhelming at first, but they are needed in order to get the help and support your child requires. I can't stress the importance of early intervention enough. Not to mention, these six steps are only the beginning. There's so much to consider when your child is officially diagnosed with autism spectrum disorder, but luckily, you don't have to face these decisions alone. With autism comes an entire community of doctors, specialists, therapists, and families just like yours who are ready and willing to welcome you with open arms.

In the next chapter, we will discuss the various health issues and conditions frequently found in children with ASD. From ADHD to sleep disturbances and intellectual disabilities, you'll learn how each one can affect your child before we move on to how to navigate the challenges that come with autism in Chapter 4.

CHAPTER 3

Various Health Issues Associated With ASD

This is a FOREVER journey with this creative, funny, highly intelligent, aggressive, impulsive, nonsocial, behavioral, oftentimes loving individual. The nurse said to me after 6 hours with him 'He is a gift' INDEED he is.

Janet Frenchette Held

I'm sure you looked at the title of this chapter and thought, "As if I didn't have enough to worry about. Now there's a chance I have to deal with more health issues on top of my child's existing autism symptoms?" Unfortunately, the answer is yes. Autism spectrum disorder is often accompanied by a number of comorbid health conditions and disorders.

But don't worry because this chapter highlights the different medical conditions often considered to be linked to autism. We will also discuss the symptoms that reveal their co-occurrence to help you understand the core issue as well. So, buckle up. This might be a bit of a bumpy ride.

Attention Deficit and Hyperactivity Disorder (ADHD)

Many people are familiar with attention deficit hyperactivity disorder, or ADHD, as it's one that plagues many children. We are used to hearing this acronym or seeing it in action whenever a super hyper child zooms past us at the grocery store or park, one of their parents chasing behind them in an attempt to calm them down. However, not many people know that ADHD and autism co-occur quite frequently.

In fact, contrary to the 6–7% of the general population diagnosed with this disorder, ADHD affects anywhere between 30–60% of those on the autism spectrum (Autism Speaks, n.d.). The symptoms of ADHD include a consistent struggle to focus on tasks, time management, staying organized, resisting impulses, remembering things, and controlling their high energy levels. These difficulties interfere with their daily lives, which is why the collection of symptoms is classified as a disorder.

The symptoms of ASD and ADHD frequently overlap, making it difficult for doctors to distinguish whether a child is actually on the spectrum. However, as you can see, it's very common for a child to have both disorders.

Sleep Disturbances

Difficulty getting a restful night's sleep can also occur in children who have autism. While some have trouble actually falling asleep, others struggle to stay asleep. As you can imagine, this might make the ability to function throughout the day and keep their emotions in check much harder.

Disturbed sleep affects many people with ASD, with as many as four out of five people on the spectrum reporting that they suffer from the effects of sleep disturbances (Autism Speaks, n.d.). Luckily, there are strategies that can help your child catch some z's, like keeping a sleep record of your child's sleeping patterns. By notating how long it took for your child to fall asleep, how often they woke up through the night, and what time they woke, you will have a helpful list to discuss with your child's doctor.

Anxiety and Depression

As if a hyper child who can't focus or get some rest wasn't enough, anxiety and depression often come into play. While Autism Speaks (n.d.) reports that 3% of children and 15% of adults, all of whom are neurotypical, have been diagnosed with some form of anxiety disorder, this percentage increases to upward of 42% for people with ASD.

An anxiety disorder presents symptoms such as a racing heart, difficulty assessing or expressing emotions, stomach aches and nausea, and muscle tightness. These symptoms can worsen over time, especially when a person's stress level rises, like when socializing with others or standing in a crowded room. If these symptoms are exhibited during these times, it's known as social anxiety. If you recall the list of indicating signs from Chapter 2, you know that socializing with others can be hard for children who have autism. This might explain why the percentage of those with ASD and co-morbid anxiety disorders is so high.

The differing percentage of the neurotypical versus the neurodivergent population is just as overwhelming when it comes to depression. The general population diagnosed with depression or depressive disorder includes 2% of children and 15% of adults, whereas 7% of children and 26% of adults with autism have been diagnosed with the same condition (Autism Speaks, n.d.).

Sadly, the large increase in depression from childhood to adulthood has to do with the worsening of symptoms. From their intellectual abilities to struggling with communication and the incessant need to mask their symptoms, it's no wonder people on the autism spectrum feel depressed.

The most frequently reported symptoms of depression include feelings of worthlessness and hopelessness, a significant decline in personal hygiene, not sleeping or sleeping too much, eating too much or not enough, chronic sadness, mood swings, long or random bouts of crying, irritability, and even suicidal ideation. Although depression can worsen over time, it doesn't mean all hope is lost. Therapy is recommended for both neurotypical and neurodivergent people if their life is impacted by depression.

Epilepsy and Seizure Disorders

According to Autism Speaks (n.d.), epilepsy affects up to 33%, or 1/3, of children and adults on the autism spectrum. Conversely, this seizure disorder affects only one to two percent of the general population. As you can see, that's a big jump. While seizures can be terrifying for the parents and people around, it's even scarier for the child as they might not understand what's going on. Even worse, if they do, by chance, recognize the sensations that occur before a seizure happens, they might not know how to explain what they're feeling in order to give their parents, friends, or teachers a fair warning.

The most common red flags for epilepsy or an impending seizure include unexplained periods of staring off into space, feeling confused for no reason, extreme headaches, and involuntary movements of the limbs or head. With that being said, some less specific signs include a disjointed sleep schedule, fatigue, and an abrupt or unexplained shift in mood.

If your child exhibits any of these symptoms, regardless of whether they have been officially diagnosed with autism spectrum disorder, it's imperative that you take them to see a neurologist as soon as possible. Epilepsy, along with other seizure disorders, is a very serious condition and causes brain damage if it's not treated; however, the condition can be treated by a trained specialist.

Intellectual Disabilities

An intellectual disability is characterized as someone with an IQ below 70 and struggles to complete day-to-day activities. This type of disability is usually diagnosed during childhood when the child is six or older. However, when the child is under six, the disability is considered a "developmental delay" and often refers to significant deficiencies in their language or cognitive thinking skills.

Although, when combined with ASD, the symptoms of intellectual disabilities might not be so black and white. While they might fall short on some skills, a child with autism might excel in others. For example, a child on the spectrum might have a deficiency in verbal skills, such as listening, talking, and understanding, but have high remarks when it comes to their nonverbal skills, like completing puzzles, writing, and drawing.

Interestingly, researchers once believed that 50–60% of children with autism had an intellectual disability; however, with the renewed diagnostic criteria, an improved source of support and education, and a better understanding of the condition, this percentage has dropped down to 20–30% (Raising Children, 2022). A perfect example of how the views on autistic children have changed would be Jacob Barnett.

When Jake was two, he began to regress. He stopped speaking and making eye contact, which, as you can imagine, terrified his parents. After being assessed, the reason as to why he was backsliding in regard to his development was given a diagnosis: autism. His future was unclear; his parents and doctor thought that he would be unable to learn since he was uncommunicative.

Initially, Jake was placed in special education classes. However, by the time he was eight, he was acing college math and science courses. Interestingly, this only happened after his mother took him out of special ed classes to homeschool him and help him follow his passions. The Indianapolis boy then went on to college, where he was a sophomore and taking honors classes in both physics and math, while he also assisted in doing scientific research and tutoring fellow students, despite only being 13 years old. During an interview with *60 Minutes*" Morley Safer, Jacob stated that autism "is the reason why I am in college and I am so successful" (Sona, 2023).

Jacob Barnett is said to have an IQ of 170, which is higher than Einstein's! In 2015, he enrolled at the Perimeter Institute for Advanced Theoretical Physics in Waterloo, Canada, to get his PhD (Sona, 2023).

Motor Skills Disorder

Children who struggle with motor skills tend to be clumsier than others, have difficulty staying balanced, and even have issues walking. Motor skills also incorporate fine motor skills, such as grasping objects, using a fork or spoon, and writing with a pencil. A deficiency in motor skills can also affect speaking, making it difficult to comprehend and understand what your child is trying to say.

There are many reasons for motor skills disorders, as some might result from muscle weakness. However, some children struggle with their motor skills and they show no issue of an irregularity in their muscles. The lack of motor skills can often be found in babies and children and can ultimately be a sign that the child has autism before the other symptoms present themselves. With 80% of people with autism having some form of motor skills deficiency, researchers believe this is one of the first indicators that may lead to an autism diagnosis (Raising Children, 2022).

One example would be that, despite attending the communication class in kindergarten, my son could not climb stairs, jump on both feet, or perform basic movements that the physiotherapist recommended for morning muscle warming. Although those incidents weren't a big deal to me, I had other more challenging matters to address, such as getting my child speech therapy to improve his vocabulary. By the age of three, he was only using around 10–20 words, and it didn't help that he was completely isolated from other children. Gradually, over time, with the aid of integrating multi-functional team therapy, he cultivated a sense of self-assurance. A crucial component that contributed to his increasing confidence was the development of his ability to balance, which allowed him to better regulate the movements of his limbs. This newfound control proved invaluable, as he could actively take part in outdoor games with his kindergarten classmates.

Conclusion

While some of these medical conditions and disorders can be scary, it's important to know that there are ways that you can help your child overcome them. Specialists and therapists can step in and give you and your child the right tools to handle the symptoms. Some of these disorders can be treated with medication or specialized therapy, such as occupational, behavioral, or even speech therapy. Remember, a child, whether they have autism or not, needs an abundance of support and patience to thrive. Try to take everything one step at a time, and before you know it, things will ultimately get better.

In the next chapter, we will discuss the challenges children with autism often face. From a mismanaged daily routine to enduring their sibling's jealousy, these issues can make your child's life much harder than it needs to be. However, challenges can be thwarted once you learn the importance of building a strong support system, which we will also go over.

CHAPTER 4

Navigating Early Challenges Faced by an Autistic Child

Since understanding and accommodation are outside of our locus of control, we can focus on our own coping mechanisms. This allows us to experience and process much more information and see patterns before others.

Joe Biel

Although you might struggle to understand what's going on with your child, it's important to remember that your son or daughter is going through their own challenges. Think of how much children learn during their formative years of life, ranging anywhere from walking to communication to socializing. Now, throw in a neurological disorder that not only makes these milestones difficult, but takes longer to process and understand their importance.

In this chapter, we will shed light on various hurdles and problems that come along with the development and day-to-day life of an autistic child.

Early Challenges in the Way of an Autistic Child

Deprived of a Healthy Family Environment

As you've seen in previous chapters, autism has a way of turning a family's life upside down. For children on the autism spectrum, their symptoms, such as sleeping disturbances and complete meltdowns, can leave an impression on their home life and the people they live with. These hallmark signs can cause frustration for parents and siblings, not to mention the children themselves.

Life before diagnosis might have been put on hold, like throwing birthday parties and family outings. These experiences—or rather, the lack of them—deprive a child with autism of a healthy family environment. Not to mention that studies have been done on how having a child with autism can affect the entire family unit. For instance, in Australia, a series of 117 parents, which consisted of 54 fathers and 107 mothers of children with autism, were given a questionnaire regarding their child's ability to function as well as their symptoms. The overall results of these questionnaires were shocking (Mathew et al., 2019):

- Both mothers and fathers reported that they felt they had a high level of efficiency when it came to their parenting style; however, they had a lower level of interest in parenting.

- Despite the mothers reporting a higher level of anxiety and stress, they also reported a higher level of overall satisfaction.

- Both mothers and fathers also showed signs of depression, which were rated higher than the country's general population.

- Based on their child's symptoms and severity, many parents reported that their child's ASD and functioning didn't affect their efficiency of being a parent, but did cause them to feel more depressed, anxious, and frustrated with the other parent.

As you can imagine, a child who is living in a home with stressed-out, frustrated, and depressed parents isn't exactly a dream. Also, it doesn't help that, according to one study, as many as 36% of those on the spectrum are children of divorce (Bahri et al., 2022). The rate has since been updated, with Psychology Today stating that as many as 80% of divorced parents have a child with autism, adding to the overall rate of 87% of parents with a special needs child (Gold Buscho, 2023).

While it doesn't matter what the actual percentage is, it's clear that parents of children with autism are overwhelmed, leading to an unhealthy home environment. Those with ASD need consistency and positive modeling when it comes to developing their skills and dealing with their symptoms; however, many don't receive these things because their parents are burnt out.

Victim of Jealousy and Hatred by Siblings

Children with autism are often an easy target for bullies, but what about when the person picking on them is their sibling? Although you might think that your other children would love nothing more than to stand up for their autistic siblings, bullying and jealousy by neurotypical siblings is actually a common struggle within families. However, it shouldn't come as much of a surprise that your other children feel some type of way toward your child with autism, as we've seen how an autism diagnosis affects families in different ways.

Interestingly, jealousy and bullying aren't the only two forms of emotion exhibited toward your autistic child by their siblings. There are actually six, including indifference, anger and frustration, being overprotective, emotional problems, jealousy, and embarrassment. Below, we will discuss how each form of these feelings is displayed (Gross, 2022):

- **Indifference:** Some children seem to be completely un-interested when it comes to spending time with their neurodivergent siblings. Whether this disinterest is caused by the difference in communication styles, especially if one of your children is nonverbal, or how the other one utilizes their play time, such as one child not showing interest in the other's current obsession. On the off chance that your neurotypical child does attempt to engage with your neurodivergent child, the amount of time they spend together is often short-lived.

- **Anger and frustration:** Having a sibling who doesn't communicate, share the same interests, or seems to be stealing much of mom and dad's undivided attention can be trying for your other children. Also, there's a chance that your other children could feel helpless, especially when your child with autism is having a meltdown, and they have no clue how to get their sibling to calm down. This feeling of overwhelm can be understandably frustrating.

- **Being overprotective:** This is the form of sibling relationship that all parents hope for, whether they have a child with special needs or not. However, we aren't just talking about being a little overprotective here. We're talking about hovering, being bossy, and watching their neurodivergent sibling like a hawk, almost as if they were a bonus parent. While an extra set of hands can be helpful, this treatment can get in the way when your child with autism is trying to strengthen certain skills, such as fine motor skills or communicating with others.

- **Emotional Issues:** If a child feels as though they are being neglected by their parents, they might display any number of emotional issues. They might isolate themselves, act out aggressively, or begin to show symptoms of depression. While they are dealing with these strong emotions, the symptoms of your neurotypical child can cause more stress within the household, causing more fractures within the family unit.

- **Jealousy:** All families deal with sibling rivalry on occasion, but this type of jealousy might appear a bit different if that green-eyed monster is directed toward a child with autism. This type of treatment can be displayed as anger, depression, regression, or isolation, but the reason for their jealousy is understandable. If you think about it, depending on a neurodivergent child's symptoms, their severity, and lack of skills, they require much of the parent's time and attention. This, in return, takes attention away from your other children, which can cause them a great deal of distress.

- **Embarrassment:** Some neurotypical siblings might feel embarrassed about their autistic siblings, especially when it comes to how they behave. This embarrassment can come into play when your child without autism is trying to socialize with their friends, all while your child with autism is obviously stimming, such as making noises, flapping their hands, or spinning around in circles. While parents might hate to see their other children be embarrassed by their neurodivergent sibling, their feelings are still valid, as many children and teenagers are worried about what their friends might think of them.

While these forms of treatment and responses can be worrisome at times, there are ways you can combat them and keep troublesome reactions at bay. For example, you can schedule an hour or so a week to give each of your children your undivided attention or become active in their favorite hobby. During this time, you can listen to what they have to say without interrupting them or invalidating their emotions regarding their relationship with their sibling. Although I know you want nothing more than to protect your child with autism, even if it's from their own sibling, this isn't the time to correct your neurotypical child or make excuses for your other child. All they want is to feel seen, heard, and understood, so make sure to give them that chance.

Mismanaged Daily Routine

If there's one thing you should know by now, it's that children with autism *really* enjoy consistency. Not only do they enjoy it, but they actually need it. A daily routine that is structured and predictable lowers their stress level, makes it easier when it comes to transitioning between tasks, keeps them focused, and provides them with a sense of comfort and security. So, with that being said, how well do you think a mismanaged daily routine affects a child with autism? The answer: not well.

This should, honestly, come as no surprise. I'm sure by now that you have dealt with the aftermath of a last-minute change in your child's routine. The results often include irritability, not being cooperative, and even a category-five meltdown. So, the best way to keep these reactions at bay is, you guessed it, a structured and predictable routine.

Difficulty Learning New Things

Compared to neurotypical children, a child with autism develops and learns at a different pace and ability. Not only do they tend to use their communication skills diversely, but they also process information differently. In fact, children on the spectrum often have difficulty processing new information or recalling details they knew previously. Whether the delay in processing is due to comprehension or overall misunderstanding, this deficiency can transfer over to other issues, such as staying organized, remaining focused, planning future tasks, and problem-solving (Zauderer, 2023).

A good example would be my son Idan's experience with riding a bike. See, unlike most kids, my child had never shown any interest in riding in those plastic toy cars, pushing himself around on a scooter, or any other typical toy that involves crashing and smashing into things around the house. We were incredibly lucky to receive an abundance of amazing gifts, including scooters, a car to ride in, and even a bike equipped with training wheels. Our strong desire was for him to sit either on his own and pedal or to be led by an adult so that he could experience the sensation of speed and the wind in his face.

Despite our insistence, he remained hesitant and chose not to even take a step closer to one of these child-sized forms of transportation. When we went to see the AC engines, as we did on a regular basis, we would make sure to point out all the cheerful kids riding their bikes to him. We had hoped it would inspire him to give his bike a try, but nothing seemed to work. And then, *bam*! Something changed.

Despite his initial reluctance to try something new, Idan finally gave in and took his first ride on a scooter at the ripe age of almost five years old. Although he didn't have a clue on how to keep himself balanced, he refused to give up and instead yelled at us every time we tried to assist him in standing or properly turning the wheel. His desire was to acquire knowledge independently and without any assistance. Even though he fell repeatedly, he remained determined and refused to give up on mastering this skill.

From this experience, I came to learn that autistic kids possess an admirable trait of being highly persistent, which is one of the many cool things about them. Even if they fail numerous times, they will persist in their efforts if they are determined to achieve something. They are very focused when it comes to achieving their goal and will not give up until they have accomplished it. For the next six months, his enthusiasm was solely focused on scooters; however, he eventually lost interest and no longer had the desire to ride them. The bike has been sitting there, waiting patiently for the day Idan will finally agree to take it out for a spin—or not.

Emotional Imbalance

Although we will discuss comorbid conditions, both mental and physical, next, it's important that we highlight the challenges surrounding a child with autism's ability to regulate their emotions. Unsurprisingly, the issues we have discussed in previous chapters and the sections above are good reasons for your child's emotional dysregulation. Between the differences in communication, information processing, and the need for a predictable schedule, an overexaggerated emotional reaction is often the only way that children on the spectrum know how to communicate their feelings and needs with those around them.

However, not to worry, all hope is not lost. Studies have actually shown that with the right support and resources, these intense emotional reactions tend to get better as the child gets older (Cibralic et al., 2019). Again, it does get better. You just have to pay attention to the key phrase here: "with the right support and resources." Luckily, we will go over how to provide these two crucial stepping stones later.

Other Rising Medical Conditions

In Chapter 3, I discussed conditions that often occur alongside autism spectrum disorder. However, some weren't mentioned that deserve to be recognized. For instance, many children on the spectrum often experience gastrointestinal issues, with the occurrence being four times more likely in children with ASD than in the rest of the general population (Nicole, 2022). The most common forms of GI complications include stomach pains, constipation, gastroesophageal reflux disease (GERD), diarrhea, and excessive gas. Some children even experience symptoms of irritable bowel syndrome (IBS).

Metabolic disorders, such as folate abnormalities and mitochondrial disorders, are often associated with autism. While the possibility of having a mitochondrial disorder occurs in only 7% of the population, the likelihood of having one is much higher when a child has autism (Nicole, 2022).

For some, a comorbid condition can be something of a scarier or worrisome variety. One of these conditions is obsessive compulsive disorder (OCD), which occurs in 17% of individuals on the autism spectrum (van Steensel et al., 2011). As repetition and recurrent behaviors are often hallmark signs of autism, they are also symptoms of OCD. Add the intrusive thoughts, which often occur in both conditions, and you have the perfect storm.

The other condition worth mentioning is child-onset schizophrenia. Did you know that autism was actually believed to be a form of schizophrenia and the result of bad parenting until 1943 (Zeldovich, 2018)? Although the criteria for diagnosis have changed exponentially over time, studies have still found there is a high rate of children with autism *and* childhood-onset schizophrenia (Rapoport et al., 2009).

Importance of Building a Strong Support Network

Now that we have discussed many of the common early challenges children with autism often face, it's time to go over the ways to combat these challenges. If you can't tell, one of the best ways is to—hint: look at the section title—build a strong support system. However, in order to build a strong support system, you need to know why it's so important.

Highly Encouraging

A strong support system is made up of you (the parents), teachers, friends, doctors, support groups, and even the family pet. Each person within this network has an important job in encouraging you and your child to keep going. Teachers can encourage your child to develop their communication and socialization skills, just like they can also help them when it comes to learning new things.

You are an excellent part of your child's support network. Not only do they rely on you to teach them and take care of their needs, but, more than likely, you are the one who's there to cheer them on. Parents can also encourage their children by rewarding them when they accomplish a goal they have struggled with or make progress in one of their developmental skills.

Friends of both yourself and your child can be a great source of encouragement, especially if they are a part of the autism community as well. Your child's friends can gently push them while still maintaining your child's boundaries to make friends with more classmates. They can also encourage your child to try new things. On the other hand, your friends can lend a supportive shoulder and compassionate ear when you're stressed out. They can listen to the issues you are struggling with and give you some solid advice on how to move forward. Some of your friends might even be nice enough to watch your child so you can get some much-needed "me time."

Eases the Pain and Stress

A strong support network can be there for you and your child when stress makes your home life a little unbearable. We all have stress in our day-to-day life and you have read how this overwhelming feeling can gain control over your family. When everything gets too much, a support group is an amazing way to fight stress.

In a support group, not only will you meet people whose lives have been impacted due to having a child with autism, but you can also get some solid advice from people who have already dealt with the same struggles you are currently facing. Your child could also meet kids who are just like them, making the overall awkwardness that comes along with making friends less obvious and more accepted.

Doctors are also a great way to ease pain and stress. Although I would never advocate for someone to medicate their child to make their life easier, many medications can help with symptoms that limit their movements or intrude on their day-to-day life.

For example, a friend of mine has a daughter on the autism spectrum and a frequent tip-toe walker. Once her daughter started kindergarten, she often complained to my friend about her ankles and legs hurting, especially after gym class. After my friend spoke to her daughter's neurologist about the complaints of pain, the doctor realized that her daughter had very stiff ankles and lacked spasticity in her leg muscles. The doctor then prescribed the young girl some muscle relaxers, and a month later, she was running around without any issues.

One of my favorite means of support when it comes to stress is—*drum roll*—the family pet. I'm sure by now that you have heard of the term "emotional support animal," but your dog, cat, guinea pig, or even goldfish doesn't have to be certified in order to make your child feel better. In fact, many therapists have incorporated animals into their treatment plans as it has a long list of proven benefits, including lower stress levels, reduced anxiety, improvement in social skills, help with communication and emotional regulation skills, decreased feelings of being judged, teaches children about empathy and responsibilities, and so much more (FCA, n.d.).

Helps With Quick Development

A child who receives early intervention tends to develop their skills much faster than one who doesn't receive this form of support. Research has proven that children with autism who not only receive an early diagnosis but also participate in early intervention treatment tend to show positive benefits and strengthen their skills on a long-term basis (NIH, 2021).

Early intervention takes many shapes, such as speech, occupational, and behavioral therapy. There is even a type of early intervention known as family training, which involves helping parents and siblings build a healthy relationship with the child and minimize symptom-caused problems at home, school, and out in public by using helpful strategies and providing family members with up-to-date information pertaining to autism.

Conclusion

As you can see, an autism diagnosis can come with many challenges, but please don't give up hope. With a strong support network, everyone in the family can have their needs met, giving your child a chance to thrive and flourish in front of our eyes.

In the next chapter, we will discuss strategies that will help your children grow. We will begin with ways to encourage your child to socialize and strengthen their communication skills. Then, we will move on to cultivating their emotional resilience and, finally, how to unlock their cognitive potential. See you there!

CHAPTER 5

Strategies to Nurture the Growth

Behavior is communication. Change the environment and behaviors will change.

Lana David

Our main goal as parents is to guide our children through the treacherous and sometimes dangerous path of life until they can navigate those paths independently. Of course, we will have to let go of their hand once they reach this metaphorical fork in the road, but you have some time until your child gets to that point.

The truth is, your child growing up is terrifying, I get it. In the back of our minds, we know there will come a day when they won't need us anymore—even though the other half of us is excited for that day. Watching as your child grows taller and learns new skills is bittersweet, but when autism comes into the picture, this transformation can get pretty scary. Secretly, you are probably wondering if they will ever make a strong support network of their own, get a job, or live independently. Well, that's where this chapter comes i n.

In this chapter, we will focus on what your child needs to become independent in the future. From developing strategies for encouraging social connections to cultivating emotional resilience and even building their confidence level, we will discuss all of those things in the sections below.

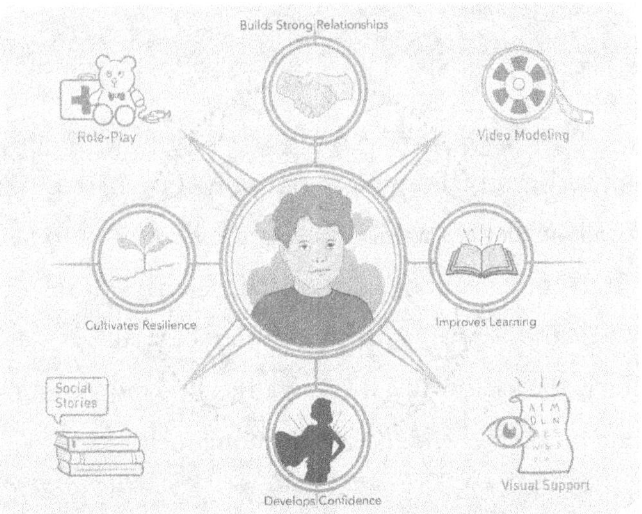

Importance of Nurturing Growth

Before we start going over the strategies to encourage your child as they grow stronger and strengthen the skills they need, let's first turn our attention to the importance of nurturing their transformation into independence. Our first stop is building strong relationships!

Builds Strong Relationships

Nurturing growth not only strengthens the relationship between child and parent, but also the relationship they have with others. It helps them meet new people and maintain friendships, especially once they become more comfortable socializing and communicating with those outside their family home.

Improves Learning

When a child feels safe and cared for, they are much calmer. This sense of security helps them to not only learn better, but also to manage challenges without losing their cool and to be more resilient. Not to mention, when you adapt what you are teaching to a child in the manner in which they learn best, such as visual aids or using audiobooks while they read, they feel more comfortable and tend to comprehend the information much easier.

Develops Confidence

By focusing on your child's strengths and talents rather than where they are lacking, they will develop more confidence. This confidence will apply in other areas of life, especially when it comes to how they handle difficult situations. For example, children and teens who feel bad about themselves tend to blow up on others when upset or angry. Whereas, a child or teen who feels confident in themselves are less likely to get upset, know they can simply walk away and will feel better about themselves because of how they handled the situation.

This confidence will also show in their school work. They will likely be less reluctant to turn in their homework because they know they tried their best. It all starts with encouragement, such as praising them for how they performed in the school play, the hard math question they answered, or how much better they are at playing the guitar.

Cultivates Resilience

Resilience is the ability to bounce back when things go wrong and to keep trying. With the challenges that many children with autism face, this quality is certainly needed so they don't just give up when life gets in the way. By being resilient, your child will be more likely to use healthy coping skills, practice positive self-talk, and feel empowered when it comes to using their problem-solving skills (Raising Children Network, 2022a).

Ways to Encourage Growth and Development

Now that you know the importance of nurturing your child's growth, it's time to find out how you can help them in doing so. Many of these techniques or strategies might be ones you have already tried, but it never hurts to have some more options.

Role-Play and Practice Play

Role-playing and practice play are a way to prepare your child for socializing with children their own age. It helps to decrease their anxiety and even reduces the chance of arguments with their peers if they don't play the same way the other child does.

Role-play comes in various forms, whether learning the rules of a game, figuring out what to say, or how to react in certain social situations. Many older children benefit from role-playing when it comes to a social problem, especially if they struggle with expressing their feelings. By coming up with a realistic scenario, you could help your child practice what to say, how to regulate their emotions, and an acceptable way to express themselves.

Practice play is often effective for younger children, as you can show them other ways to play with their toys, similar to how their peers would play. For example, you could focus on imaginary play, such as playing house. You could show your child how to cradle the baby doll, swaddle them in a blanket, feed them a bottle, and put them to sleep. While this might sound like you are trying to make your child more "neurotypical" or change who they are, remember that you are trying to help them learn to play with others. It also teaches them that there are many ways to play with the same toy, which will carry over later in life when they learn that there are many ways to figure out a problem.

Video Modeling

Although some videos for children can seem redundant or downright annoying, some can actually be helpful for your children when it comes to strengthening their skills. Video modeling is used to teach a child with autism a positive replacement behavior or how to employ a new skill.

This technique is to record yourself or a family member practicing a skill or behavior, and then the child watches the recording and copies the action. A large range of topics can be taped, such as waving, communicating with friends, or how to act when angry with someone.

Social Stories

For those who have never heard of social stories or have heard of them but don't know what they are, social stories are scenarios that help autistic or neurodivergent children how to handle certain social situations. They are designed to help your child learn how to control their emotions and behave properly while also helping to develop their social skills. They also help your child develop their nonverbal communication skills as they learn to understand the meaning behind body language, facial expressions, and the importance of eye contact.

These stories are scripts tailored to your child's area of concern and are written to match your child's skills and age so they can understand. The scripts all point out the same things despite the scenario: the details of the situation, what would normally happen in this particular situation, and how the child should behave.

Visual Support

Visual aids, such as pictures or slides, can help your child develop, strengthen, and even recall the skills they have learned so far. If your child knows how to read already, these forms of support can even include words or sentences to help them remember.

This technique can be used to come up with topics to discuss with others, like what to ask Grandma when you visit her. Or, you could use them to explain the rules and concepts of a game.

Appreciation and Gratitude

As we all know, a little appreciation and gratitude go a long way. However, you might be asking, how do these two things help your child to grow their skills? Well, for one, gratitude and appreciation help your child develop empathy, understand how those around them are feeling, and teach them to be kind. Plus, there's the benefit of these two qualities making you feel happier and more enjoyable to be around, as researchers have found that being appreciative and gracious toward others makes us healthier, sleep better, and have higher self-esteem (ICT, 2017).

You can help your child develop these two things by modeling these behaviors, being consistent with using your manners (especially saying "please" and "thank you"), and involving your child when you are helping others. You could also work appreciation and gratitude into your child's playtime through role-playing and practice play.

Conclusion

Nurturing your child as they grow, not only older, but also strengthening their skills is a crucial part of parenting. While it benefits them in many ways, like helping them make friends and be more empathetic toward others, it also helps them to make their feelings and needs known. Your support throughout the process will help them become more confident and resilient, which we want most for our children.

In the next chapter, we will continue to discuss how to help your child grow, but in a different way. Instead, you will learn how to help your child unlock their inner strengths and use them to their advantage while also using this chance to celebrate the areas in which they excel.

Unlocking the Inner Strengths

For autistic individuals to succeed in this world, they need to find their strengths and the people that will help them get to their hopes and dreams.

Bill Wong

I know we have spoken a lot about symptoms, meltdowns, and sensory issues; however, that's not all that children with autism have to offer. Just like every other person on this Earth, individuals on the spectrum have their own unique talents. Whether through art, music, technology or simply having an impressive memory bank, autistic children's strengths certainly outweigh their weaknesses. Sometimes, though, those strengths haven't been discovered yet, and they might need your help to find and embrace them.

This chapter will focus on recognizing and celebrating special talents that can help build your child's self-esteem and confidence. This, in turn, will assist in fostering independence and self-advocacy in your autistic child.

Strengths of an Autistic Child

Children on the autism spectrum might not learn the same way as their neurotypical peers, but that doesn't mean they don't have their own set of unique strengths. Sadly, once society learns that an individual has autism, the person is often discounted as "damaged" or "deficient." Many people don't think about the fact that an autistic child's talents might actually outshine their own, but in different ways, which only furthers the stigma surrounding autism.

Exceptional Memory

While many children, and even adults, with autism struggle with their short-term memory, this doesn't seem to affect their long-term memory. In fact, research has found that, compared to the neurotypical person's ability to remember events that occurred four to six years ago, a person on the spectrum can often recall events that happened much further back (Crespi, 2016).

Some individuals on the spectrum even have a photographic memory, meaning that while they struggle to remember someone's name or profession, they can recall some very minute details of something they read long ago. They may also be able to recall certain facts from a long time ago, such as their phone number from first grade or their best friend from kindergarten's birthday.

Unparalleled Creativity

Not only have researchers found a strong link between autism and creative ability, but they have also discovered that this strength can be used for other aspects of life, such as problem-solving (University of East Anglia, 2015). With this finding in mind, it's no wonder why so many scientists, artists, and philosophers throughout history are believed to be on the spectrum.

The same researchers who found this link stated they conducted studies intending to prove that people with autism should be thought of as different rather than having deficits (Goode & Shinkle, 2021). Their brains are "wired" differently than those of a neurotypical person, which allows them to think and express themselves more visually or artistically. Parents, siblings, and teachers should celebrate and encourage this strength.

Detail-Oriented

Besides a spectacular long-term memory and unequivocal creative mind, people on the spectrum are unique in their ability to recall and point out small details. This strength is all due to how their brain is wired and processes information. Since those with autism tend to obsess over routine and things staying the same, they actually become more attentive when they feel something is amiss. This ability allows someone on the spectrum to focus on a task better and accomplish it faster and more efficiently than someone without the disorder (Szalavitz, 2012).

Unique Way of Thinking

Much like how a person with autism communicates and socializes differently, they also think in a more unique way compared to neurotypical individuals. In fact, the way they think, often referred to as "logical thinking," is one of the main characteristics of the disorder.

Logical thinking refers to how the brain uses facts rather than intuition to come up with a conclusion. Those on the spectrum are also said to use what's known as "bottom-up" thinking, where they "use details to build concepts," as opposed to how neurotypical individuals think, where they build the concept and then add details (Lovering, 2022).

Other research has shown that there are two types of thinking: neurotypical individuals tend to lean toward type one, while neurodivergent and autistic individuals tend to lean toward type two. For example, those with autism tend to be more deliberate with their decisions and base their conclusions on rules, whereas those considered to be neurotypical tend to be more intuitive and base their conclusions on experiences they have dealt with (Brosnan et al., 2016).

The main consensus throughout each study is that, although it may take longer for a neurodivergent person to filter through all of the unnecessary and sensory information, they are less likely to miss a minor detail. It should also be mentioned how a person on the autism spectrum's thinking affects their interpretation of literal language. With all of the idioms and sayings in the world, it can be difficult for those with autism to interpret the statements, causing them to take the sayings literally. This is one reason you have to be clear and concise when speaking with someone with autism, as it will avoid any misunderstandings and confusion.

Conclusion

Once you have recognized your child's strengths, it's crucial that you encourage and support them so they continue to use them.

Although these traits might not be a "use it or lose it" type of deal, they can help them in the future when it comes to their education and career.

Speaking of education, in the next chapter, we will discuss how to build connections with your child's school district, teachers, and special education programs to ensure they receive the academic support they need. We will also go over how to establish an effective Individualized Education Plan (IEP) and how teachers can be a means of support for your child. Now, hurry along to the next chapter; the school bell is about to ring!

CHAPTER 7

Building Bridges at School

For every three years your child is in public school, you can expect one exceptional teacher, one mediocre teacher, and one teacher who makes your life miserable.

Rick Seward

Trusting that your children will be safe at school should be a given, but times have changed since you and I were students. While many students are now "woke," as the kids say, that doesn't mean there still aren't bullies walking through the halls.

Besides worrying about your child's safety, you also have to worry about whether they receive a quality education despite their autism symptoms and delay in processing information. You might not know where to turn when it comes to your child's education and making sure they are included, but this is where this book comes in handy.

In this chapter, we will focus on creating an effective Individualized Education Plan (IEP), collaborating with teachers and school staff, promoting inclusion, and bullying prevention. School might be scary for both you and your child, but it doesn't have to be.

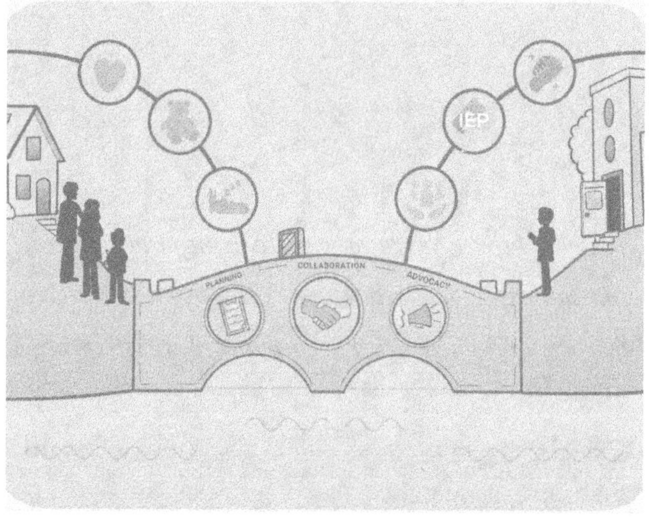

Steps to Create an Effective Individualized Education Plan

An IEP works as a roadmap for your child's education. It lays out the support your child needs, ranging from extra time on tests to the ability to take breaks, even if supplemental aids are needed, like a classroom assistant. These forms of support and extra resources are there to ensure your child is successful throughout their academic career.

Although coming up with an IEP can take a little bit of time, remember that *you* have the ability to make this process run smoother on your end by doing the following things:

- **Compile information:** Before the date for your child's IEP meeting arrives, make sure you have all of your ducks in a row. Gather every bit of information you can regarding your child's needs, pertaining to both personal and educational data. This could be previous grade cards, reports from teachers, testing results, and even a letter from your child's occupational, behavioral, and speech therapist, specialists, or previous special education program directors. Having this information in your toolbelt will ensure that you have everything you need and won't have to rush to find it if it's, by chance, needed.

- **Articulate your child's needs and strengths:** As I previously stated, you know your child best. You know what topics or skills they need the most help with and where they are lacking, whether socially, academically, or physically. Take this opportunity to highlight these needs, as an IEP can get your child the support they require and possibly even the help you can't get on your own. For example, many schools have occupational and speech therapists on staff, as they are aware that some families may not be able to afford this form of intervention, or it's not covered by their insurance. This means that an IEP is one way parents can ensure their child gets the help they truly need.

Oftentimes, the school tends to focus on where the child needs help rather than what skills they excel at. Make sure to keep this in mind when you head into the meeting. It will come in handy for the next step.

- **Jot down your ideal goals for your child's education:** The IEP meetings can get a bit stressful, so to make sure that you remember everything you need to say or input you'd like to add, jot down any goals you have for your child pertaining to this school year beforehand. This could be anywhere from getting their reading level to where it should be or learning a certain amount of words if they are nonverbal. Taking the time to write these goals down ensures that you don't feel rushed, have time to think it over, and can discuss them with your child's other parent and doctors.

- **Request a copy of the draft:** By receiving your own copy of the IEP, you are given the chance to compare it to your child's previous learning plan, if they have one, and ensure that you know what's written in the event that the guidelines aren't being followed. While many schools enforce IEPs with an iron fist, there are those that seem to be more lenient. Having your own copy gives you the ability to point out where your child's teacher is lacking when it comes to following the plan so you can continue to advocate for your child and their future. Now, I'm not saying that your child's school may be one that ignores a child's academic needs when it comes to support, just that there are some that tend to slip through the cracks.

- **Never stop advocating for your child:** Pertaining to the last point, it's crucial that you never stop advocating for your child. Remember, your child is *your* responsibility and priority, so don't let anyone pressure you to change your mind regarding their needs and the type of help they need. Don't be afraid to speak up if you feel their IEP isn't being honored, as it's your right to make sure both the school administration and your child's teachers are following the plan in place. When it comes to your child's future, don't let any system—big or small—silence you. You are a mama or papa bear, so growl as loud as you need to in order to get the support your child needs.

Ways Teachers Can Support an Autistic Child

A teacher's job is to teach and support students as they navigate their way through the lessons. With that being said, it's important to ensure that your child's teacher implements and applies your child's IEP while they are in the classroom. So, when your child starts school, there are a few things that you should look into:

Inclusive Classrooms

Check if your child is in an inclusive classroom. Do they teach right out of the book or use the students' interests, strengths, and skills to keep the lesson interesting and understandable? Do they use alternative methods or accommodate a student's needs if a child lacks certain skills? For example, do they allow students to use a computer for their assignments if they lack the fine motor skills needed to write? Do they encourage students to take a break if they get overwhelmed or frustrated?

Bully Prevention Measures

Another thing you want to look into when your child is assigned to a new teacher is their stance on bullying. Does the teacher explain the expectations for the student's behavior? Are they observant when it comes to how their students treat one another? How do they tend to react when a student is teasing or being aggressive with another student? Does the teacher make the classroom feel like a safe environment, meaning your child could come to them if they were being bullied?

A Comfortable Learning Environment

Similar to the topic above, it's important to look into the learning environment your child will be stationed in for seven to eight hours of the day. If the room is unorganized and chaotic, they will probably have difficulty learning or focusing on the task in front of them. Also, ask your child what their daily schedule looks like. Is it predictable or do the students tend to run the classroom?

Conclusion

Although making decisions about school, such as whether to go mainstream, stick with special education classes, or which accommodations in their IEP are enough to make anyone's head spin, I assure you that you got this in the bag. You know what's best for your child, and if you need help making a decision, there are plenty of people to guide you toward the right decision. You could speak with your child's therapists, teachers, or the school's special education director, but it's still ultimately up to you in the end.

Only you can be certain of the type of support your child needs when it comes to their education, and that's because you are the person who spends the most time with them. Parents are the ones who know the best way to teach their children new things, such as using audiobooks while they read, utilizing visual aids to teach them how to do something step by step, or if they do their best work independently in a quiet location. Parents are also the most knowledgeable about the signals their child gives when they need to step away and take a break. That's why a child's primary caregivers are such an instrumental part in helping the school and teachers create an effective and manageable IEP.

Although coming up with an Individualized Education Plan can take a little bit of time, remember that *you* can make this process run smoother on your end by doing the following things:

- **Compile all the information you need.** This includes reports, evaluation results, and any recommendations from your child's various therapists.

- **Articulate your child's needs and strengths.** You know what your child needs, as well as what they excel at, so make sure they are mentioned.

- **Jot down your ideal goals for your child's education.** Think about these goals beforehand so you don't forget during the IEP meeting.

- **Request a copy of the draft.** It's your right to get a copy of the IEP's draft, not only so you can compare it to the previous years, but also to ensure that it's being followed.

- **You have a voice; don't be afraid to use it.** It's your responsibility to be an advocate for your child. Never be afraid to stand up for your child's needs or right to receive a good education.

Whether your child is in special education classes or you decide to go mainstream, school is a big transition for your child. In the next chapter, we will discuss how you can help your child make transitions and accept changes, making the process much smoother and less likely to result in a full-on meltdown. Keep reading because you aren't going to want to miss this information!

CHAPTER 8

Managing Transitions and Challenges

Autistic people are capable of doing amazing things when they are given the right tools and opportunities.

Dr. Temple Grandin

Difficulty dealing with changes and transitions has been mentioned many times in this book, as it's one of the main issues children with autism face. No one likes change, whether they are on the spectrum or not, but a neurodivergent child has a certain distaste for it and they aren't afraid to show how they feel. Sometimes, this aversion toward transitions might come across as reluctance, and other times, it might result in a full-on category-5 meltdown.

Well, in this chapter, we will discuss some ways to help your child cope with changes and transitions. We will also go over how to handle meltdowns and sensory overload, as well as how to address their behavioral challenges.

Why Is Transitioning Difficult for an Autistic Child?

By now, I'm sure you have gotten to the point where you grit your teeth whenever you know it's time to transition from one task to another. You know there will be some pushback and reluctance, and you are just wondering why your child acts this way every time they have to put their toys away so they can take a bath. Well, you're not alone, as many parents find themselves asking the same question.

Well, according to child psychologist David Anderson, there's a reason why you often find yourself negotiating with your child when it's time to put down the video game controller and eat dinner. Besides switching tasks taking a large amount of energy, children on the spectrum find transitioning especially hard because they're "transitioning from a preferred activity—something we like doing—to something that they need to do" (Martinelli, 2021). The combination of energy usage and reluctance to stop doing what *they* want to do can cause your child to feel overwhelmed by their emotions, thus prompting them to react in any number of ways. Some children might scream and act defiantly, some might cry, and some might have a meltdown. However, there are ways that you can combat these reactions, which you will find below.

Ways to Make Transition Easier

When you first start implementing these strategies, don't be surprised if there is a bit of pushback. If you think about it, these helpful tips are, in fact, a change for the child. However, over time, they will get used to them, and things will start running much smoother.

Prepare Them for a Transition Beforehand

One strategy that I have found to be particularly useful is giving my child a timeline. For instance, if he is drawing or coloring and needs to shower in half an hour, I let him know that he has 30 minutes to finish what he is doing. Then, I tell him what needs to be done once that time is over.

When half of the time is over, I let him know. I'll say, "Hey buddy, how's your picture coming? You have about 15 more minutes until you have to get in the shower, okay?" Then, I do the same thing when only five minutes are left, letting him know that his playtime is almost over. When the time has elapsed, I let him know it's time to pick up whatever toys he is using and do what needs to be done. This strategy not only prepares him for what to expect, but also teaches him to manage his time.

Use Visual Timers and Charts to Remind Them

While some parents might find a spoken reminder useful, other parents might prefer to use visuals, like a poster board with images next to the written tasks and the time they need to be completed. You could even get a digital clock and place it next to the board so everything is in one place and much easier to follow.

Some parents have even found the use of timers to be effective. Technology makes this strategy easily accessible, as there are many phone or tablet apps that implement a child-friendly timer. You can set the timer to go off when it's time to transition to the next task, and the app makes it easier for them to see how much time they have left to finish what they are doing. In my research, I have found a decent-sized list of visual timers that are actually recommended for children on the spectrum (Lightner, 2022):

- **Visual Timer:** Available on iTunes, this app is simple in nature and its reviews state that it's very helpful when setting up and keeping track of time. You can also create a preset schedule for the alarm and set it to dark mode, so it's easy on the eyes.

- **Kids Timer:** Created by the company Skywise and available on Google Play, this timer is said to help children learn about the concept of time. It allows your child to estimate how much time a task will take and set the timer (or you can set it for them) and shows a large, blue clock ticking down the time. When the timer is nearing the end, it turns red, signaling that the alarm is about to go off and to get ready to transition to the next task.

- **Visual Countdown Timer:** Created by the developers at Fehners Software and available on iTunes *and* the Google Play Store, this visual timer was made with children in mind. It allows the child to choose a picture of their liking and set the timer. As time passes by, a small pie slice of the image disappears. Once the picture is completely gone, the timer goes off.

- **Happy Kids Timer:** Developed by Kids Smart Zone and available on the Google Play Store, this visual timer actually includes daily chores that need to be done as a way to encourage children to be independent. The app has glowing reviews, with many parents stating that they love the use of color and animations. Also, the app was designed with kids in mind, as the intention is for them to carry the tablet or phone with them while they use the app and complete their chores.

- **Mr Bomb and Friends 2:** This particular visual count-down has rave reviews online, but many parents warn that it can be a bit distracting for younger children and might get them a little too excited if used before bedtime. Developed by the company Rule of Fun and available on Google Play, this app uses cartoon characters to display the time as it counts down.

Reward Them for Their Achievements

As your child gets used to these strategies and the reluctance starts to fade a little, show them that you appreciate all their hard work. Reward them for their achievements, whether following the schedule every day for a week or not throwing a tantrum as they change activities. The reward doesn't have to be huge, but could be as simple as going out for ice cream or letting them choose a family activity for that weekend.

Rewards encourage them to continue using positive behavior and communicate their needs rather than lashing out. You could even create a reward chart, where you place a sticker or gold star for each day they transitioned between tasks without pushback.

Keep Guiding and Motivating Them

As I stated before, there will be some reluctance when you start to utilize strategies to help with transitions. Remember that children with autism enjoy repetition and crave consistency, so you have to be predictable when implementing whatever tips you choose. With that being said, that doesn't mean that there won't be days that your child puts up a fight. They will still have bad days where they don't want to get with the program, and that's to be expected. However, what's important is that you keep doing what you are doing and motivate them to follow along.

If you are using a reward chart, this will help to keep them motivated as they see how many more days they have until they receive their reward. By no means should you use withholding their daily gold star as a threat if they don't comply, but this will encourage them to try again the next day. It will also teach them that there are consequences for their actions, which is an important lesson to learn as a child.

Stay Connected to Them

Even though you are trying to help your child become more independent, you should still make an effort to stay connected with them throughout this process. If they are having a bad day, speak to them calmly and find out what's going on. You never know; you might be surprised by their answer. Your child could feel frustrated with the new strategies you are implementing, feel rushed all the time, or feel like these new techniques are meant to be punishments.

Make sure to listen to what your child says, validate their feelings, and figure out alternate ways to help them transition without the negative emotions attached. Many times, utilizing new tips and strategies is trial and error. That's why I have given you various options to try so you can figure out which ones work best for you, your child, and your family as a whole.

Conclusion

As I stated at the beginning of this chapter, no one likes change. It's new and uncomfortable, and you're never sure of how or if it's actually going to work. However, with the right support and staying consistent, you can reduce the stress your child experiences due to a sudden change of plans or transitioning from one task to another. This, in turn, should also help reduce the severity and frequency of their meltdowns and sensory overload.

In the next chapter, it's all about you: the parent. You will learn some effective ways to manage the stress you are feeling and ways that you can find support for the needs you have been neglecting for quite some time. Last but not least, we will discuss the dreaded caregiver burnout and the symptoms you should look out for. So, take some time and think about yourself for once as we move on to the next chapter.

CHAPTER 9

The Parent's Emotional Well-Being

Autism doesn't come with an instruction manual, but it comes with a parent who will never give up.

Laura Tisoncik

Although I know some days are so busy that you can barely function by the time you lay your head down on your pillow at night, it's important to remember that you, too, are a human being. You have needs and wants that must be fulfilled, just like your children. The only difference is that you might be more attuned to their needs than your own—and that isn't a good thing. In fact, ignoring your emotional, mental, and physical needs is the fastest way to burn out, which many parents of autistic and special needs children experience.

In this chapter, I will emphasize the importance of self-care and resilience for parents and caregivers by offering strategies for managing stress, finding strength, and prioritizing their well-being by balancing parenting and personal life. While I understand that these strategies are easier said than done, you must take care of yourself. As the old saying goes, "You can't pour from an empty cup."

Ways to Manage Stress

Stress will always be a factor in your life, but that's just how it goes. We need stress to motivate us to get up in the morning and go to work, as our bills and groceries aren't going to pay for themselves. Even from a scientific perspective, stress can be helpful for you.

When you feel stressed out, your adrenal glands start pumping out dopamine, which makes your heart pump faster and pushes more oxygen to the brain and through the bloodstream. In turn, you feel more alert, are able to focus, and experience an increase in energy. Before society became what it is today, stress kept humans alive.

However, life has changed so much since cavemen walked the Earth. We no longer hunt prehistoric creatures to feed our families or climb trees to hide from animals that wish to eat us. Instead, we rush from work to the grocery store, and then run home to cook dinner, hoping that the dishes and homework will be done before we have to force the kids to shower. So, while stress can be a good thing, too much of it can be detrimental to our health.

Meditate Regularly

Practiced for centuries due to its ability to calm down the anxious, stress-filled, and overwhelmed souls of the world, meditation is one of the best ways to relax and clear your mind. It has a long list of benefits, ranging from an increase in self-awareness to slowing down your heart rate to even lowering your blood pressure. Not to mention, it gets you out of your head, away from your thoughts, and relaxes your body all at the same time. Who wouldn't enjoy that?

Although it takes practice to keep your mind from wandering and focusing back on your breathing, it's not complicated, and it doesn't require any specialized equipment. There are many forms of meditation that you can practice, including yoga, guided meditation, and mindfulness meditation. If you don't know where to start or feel strange sitting in silence, you could utilize a phone app, such as Headspace or Calm, or find one that catches your interest on YouTube. In essence, it doesn't matter how you choose to meditate as long as you set some time aside each day to do it.

Practice Positive Self-Talk

Did you know that talking to yourself in a positive manner has been scientifically proven to improve your self-esteem, lower your stress levels, reduce the symptoms of anxiety and depression, help with chronic pain, promote a healthy body image, and motivate you to keep going in hard times (Healthdirect, 2022)? Isn't it crazy that something as simple as talking kindly to yourself can have so many positive benefits for you and your life? But, as many things are in life, it's much easier said than done.

In order to change your perspective from "glass half-empty" to "glass half-full," you have to do one thing: stop talking to yourself negatively. The first step is to pay attention to what you are saying to yourself and pause for a moment. Ask whether what you're saying is true—and a little hint here, it's not. Then, challenge that negative thought and turn it around. For example, instead of saying, "I'm such a loser. I can't do anything right," try saying, "Things didn't work out today, and that's okay. I'll keep trying until I figure it out."

Repeat Positive Affirmations

One of the best forms of self-care is positive affirmations, as they challenge negative thoughts, motivate you to keep working toward your goal, and even boost your self-esteem. Despite "positive affirmations" being a buzzword, not many people understand what they are or how to use them to benefit their mental health.

Positive affirmations are phrases that you say to yourself on a daily basis, or you can write them down and place them where you can see them throughout the day. They often start with an "I" followed by a statement, such as "I am a loving mother" or "I am a strong person and can deal with anything that comes my way." Repeating these statements to yourself throughout the day, especially when you are feeling down or questioning your abilities, can remind you of who you are and give you a little mood booster.

Do Breathing Exercises

As someone who has practiced this technique whenever I'm stressed out, overwhelmed, or just don't have my head in the game, I swear by breathing exercises. They can get you out of your head and back into the present moment just by doing something that we do automatically. How awesome is that?

You can try many different types of breathing exercises; you just have to find which one works best for you. Before I go over some of the most common exercises, I will let you know that the first steps to almost all the different techniques are the same: find a comfortable place to sit or lie down that's quiet and close your eyes. No special equipment is needed, just you and your lungs.

Below, I have given you a quick overview of five different exercises for you to check out and see which one you prefer (Ankrom, 2021):

- **Alternate-nostril breathing:** Using your pointer finger, block off one of your nostrils. Now, just to be clear, don't shove your finger in your nose to block it; just press the nostril close. Then, breathe normally through the open nostril, then alternate.

- **Lion's breath:** This exercise is a little strange, but it's said to help lower your stress level and relax the muscles in your face. In a seated position, lean forward slightly and place your hands on the floor or your knees. Then, spread your fingers as wide as you can while inhaling through your nose. Next, open your mouth, stick out your tongue, and try to stretch it all the way down to your chin. With your mouth still open and tongue out, exhale as hard as you can and say "ha," pushing the breath and sound out from the bottom of your abdomen. Then, breathe normally for a little bit and do the lion's breath a few more times.

- **4-7-8 breathing:** In a seated position, place the tip of your tongue against the roof of your mouth, directly behind your front teeth. Then, breathe out through your mouth, making a "whooshing" noise. Next, close your mouth and breathe in and out through your nostrils for four seconds before holding your breath for seven seconds. Lastly, open your mouth again, your tongue still touching the roof and sitting behind your teeth, and exhale for eight seconds.

- **Belly breathing:** In a seated or lying position, place one hand on your upper chest, preferably slightly under your collar bone, and the other hand just below your ribcage. Then, relax all the muscles in your stomach, meaning try not to clench your muscles. Once your abdominal muscles are relaxed, inhale slowly through your nose as you focus on how your stomach feels as you breathe in and out. This specific exercise is said to reduce your anxiety and stress levels.

- **Resonance breathing:** Also known as "coherent breathing," this exercise is supposed to help reduce your anxiety and calm you down when you're overwhelmed. Different from the other four, for this breathing exercise, you will lie down in a quiet place. Then, with your mouth closed, breathe in through your nose slowly as you count to six and exhale for another six seconds. Continue practicing this exercise for 10 minutes, and afterward, lie still and pay attention to how your body is feeling. If you still aren't relaxed, repeat the steps until you start to feel better.

Spend Time in Nature

When was the last time you actually went outside and enjoyed it? Better yet, when was the last time you went outside and enjoyed nature *alone*? While it's great to take your children to the park to play or go for a walk, as parents, we often spend most of our time chasing them around and making sure they don't get hurt. That's not very relaxing, right? So, do yourself a favor and find a sitter or have your spouse watch the kids for as little as half an hour while you take a nice walk. Go to the nearest park and take a relaxing walk along the nature trails, inhaling as much fresh air as possible.

You could even find a quiet area under the trees and meditate for a little bit, practicing two strategies on this list at the same time. Close your eyes and inhale deeply, feeling the fresh air fill your lungs as you run your fingers through the lush green grass beneath you. Clear your mind and listen to the sounds of the birds flying over your head or the crickets chirping a few feet away. Focus on where you are at that moment, and you'll be amazed by how refreshed you feel once you open your eyes and rejoin the rest of the world.

Read Motivational Books

Books meant to inspire and motivate us do an amazing job at doing just that. They lift us from the dark hole we have found ourselves in and push us to keep going. Clearly, since you chose to read this book, you have very good taste and know all about ways to build your confidence in all facets of life. However, pride aside, motivational books can work wonders when you want to relax and look on the brighter side of life with a fresh and more positive perspective.

But what if you're not interested in delving into the world of *Chicken Noodle Soup* books? Well, that's simple. You could honestly read whatever type of book you enjoy as long as it makes you feel relaxed. Or, maybe you aren't a big reader. There's a solution for that as well: movies. There is a *huge* amount of movies that you could watch if you need to be inspired; just point the remote at the screen and press play.

Ways to Find Support for Yourself

Now that you know some ways to manage your stress, although there are literally hundreds of other examples out there, it's time to find out how to find support for yourself. Yes, I'm sure you are sitting there and asking why *you*, of all people, need support.

I'm sure you also probably think that you have this parenting, adulting, and self-care thing down by now, but do you really? Are you truly happy with how your life is now or do you find yourself wishing that you had someone there for you like you're there for everyone else? Let me tell you the secret: You aren't the only parent who feels this way. Day after day, we give every bit of energy and focus to others who aren't us. By the end of the day, we just want to relax because we know we must do the same thing tomorrow. Sure, we are taking care of the ones we love, but who is taking care of you?

As you ponder that question, let's discuss some of the helpful ways that you can find support for *you*. Believe me, you'll thank me later.

Talk to Your Close Friends and Family Members

Your family and friends know you the best. They have seen you rise above your challenges, and they have also seen you at your worst. This is one of the reasons that they make such a great form of support. Although they might not be able to give you sound medical advice, they can remind you of how far you have come. They can also tell you stories of how you overcame an obstacle, sometimes reminding you of a time you forgot long ago.

Close friends are also great for lending a shoulder to cry on or a compassionate ear when you need to vent. You don't even have to talk about anything related to autism, children, work, or your marriage. You could just talk to hear your own voice, reassuring you that it's still there after all this time. Also, people who have known us for years always tend to know how to make us smile—and who couldn't use a good laugh when they're stressed?

Consult a Counselor

If you feel like you've tried everything and are still feeling mentally, emotionally, and physically drained, it may be time that you consult with a therapist. They can be an objective outsider, giving you advice you haven't thought of yet because, as you know, it's hard to see clearly when you are standing in the middle of a storm. A counselor can guide you through the craziness life has thrown your way and even refer you toward support groups that may help you.

A therapist could also recognize the signs of depression or an anxiety disorder and refer you to a psychiatrist. Although I'm sure you are tired of dealing with doctors and different types of therapists by now, remember that that's one of the reasons why you feel so terrible. You never put yourself first; believe it or not, medication management and treatment could get you back to the person you used to be.

Find Helpful Caregivers for Your Child

Every parent needs a night off every once in a while, whether they have a child with special needs or not. I mean, we spend all week taking care of everyone else's needs, day in and day out, making sure they are happy. We get our work done to appease our bosses, cook dinners our family loves, and shuttle everyone to school and extracurricular activities as if we were a taxi cab. Moms and dads around the world break their backs all day, every day, to ensure there are clothes on their children's backs and food in their stomachs, yet we tend to forget about ourselves and our need for a little break.

This is where a helpful hand in the form of a caregiver or babysitter comes in. Having someone you trust to sit and watch your child while you get some alone time or go on a date with your significant other is a much-needed necessity, especially when you have a child with autism. Give yourself time to be alone, hang out with friends, or participate in a deep conversation with your spouse; you deserve it. Of course, as I said, make sure you leave your child with someone *they* know and trust, not just you. Make sure the sitter is well aware of your child's symptoms, diagnosis, and how they can contact you while you are gone if a problem arises.

Join Autism Support Groups

Never underestimate the power of an autism support group. Sure, you may be mentally exhausted from thinking, researching, and talking about how this disorder affects you, your child, and your family as a whole, but isn't it nice to know that you aren't the only person who feels this way? The good thing is that you don't just hear other parents' experiences with autism spectrum disorder, as there are so many benefits. For example, you can make connections within the autism community; learn new strategies to help manage your child's symptoms that you hadn't heard of before; and give advice on therapies or specialists who listen and truly look out for their patients.

Another benefit of support groups is that you will feel heard as you share your experiences—both good and bad—with your autistic child, as many of the people in the group have been there, done that, and moved past it. Your frustrations, worries, and proud moments won't fall on deaf ears because you know these people are cheering for you and your family. Also, there's a chance you could meet someone who could help with respite care or a trusted individual who takes care of children with special needs for an extended amount of time, often ranging from hours to even a few days, when you need a break.

The Red Flags of Caregiver Burnout

Although I don't want to dive too deeply into caregiver burnout, failing to discuss the symptoms of caregiver burnout would be neglectful on my part. In Chapter 4, you read about how having a child on the spectrum can cause parents to feel overwhelmed, stressed out, and even depressed. Well, those uncomfortable emotions, along with the physical exhaustion that many parents already deal with, will ultimately lead to a major case of burnout.

Being a parent alone can make one feel burnt out, but some studies present how autism being in the mix can increase the likelihood. One study states that 90% of parents or primary caregivers of children on the autism spectrum feel overburdened by their child's condition and symptoms, and 54% reportedly showed signs of severely unhealthy psychological and mental well-being (Keller & Honig, 2004). I don't know about you, but those percentages scare me. I would never want to find myself in that position, although there have been times that I have been on the verge of my own meltdown, and I wouldn't want you to start losing your grip, either.

With that being said, let's go over the signs and symptoms of caregiver burnout that you need to look out for (Autism Therapy Group, 2021):

- You're having a hard time controlling your emotions.

- You either avoid making future plans or are constantly rescheduling them.

- You have lost interest in your hobbies or show disinterest in anything you used to enjoy.

- You keep canceling or can't find the time to go to your own doctor's appointments.

- You are either sleeping too much or not enough.

- You find yourself feeling emotionally numb, constantly cynical toward others, or have a strong sense of resentment toward your children and/or spouse.

- Your level of exhaustion has made it difficult to think or physically take care of yourself.

- You feel as if you're always on edge, liable to snap at anyone for even a minor inconvenience.

- You have started to abuse drugs or alcohol in order to cope with your stress.

After you look over these symptoms, you are probably thinking that this list could easily describe the aftermath of a hard day. However, if these signs last for more than a day or two, then it might be time that you take a break and do some after-care. Hopefully, you haven't reached this point yet, and with the lists I have provided above, I hope you never get the chance to experience burnout.

Conclusion

Life can get pretty hectic sometimes, that I know for sure. However, no one has ever been so busy that they couldn't spare even five minutes for themselves so they could catch their breath. If you can't find some time for yourself, then it's time that you require your "me time," no longer making it an option. Pull out that handy dandy calendar, which I'm sure we both know you depend on to keep life moving as smoothly as possible and schedule your me time where everyone can see it. Make sure you communicate to everyone that during this time, you are "incommunicado." Put your phone on airplane mode so no one disturbs your peace. This time is for you to relax so you can get back to being, well, you again. Enjoy it; you deserve it.

Once you have taken some time for yourself, you can turn your focus onto the next step: how to help strengthen the bond between your autistic child and their siblings. In the next chapter, we will go over some practical tips on how to do just that, as well as some strategies to make your family unit stronger as a whole.

CHAPTER 10

Thriving Together—Siblings and Family Dynamics

When a family focuses on ability instead of disability, all things are possible... Love and acceptance is key. We need to interact with those with autism by taking an interest in their interests.

Amanda Rae Ross

The relationship between siblings is like no other. Brothers and sisters would gladly hurt another person if they were to hurt their sibling, as only they are allowed to do so. They would kill for their brother or sister but refuse to share the last cookie with them. They would also gladly donate their kidney to their sibling but would rather cut off their arm than let their brother or sister use their phone charger. The point is that sibling relationships can be weird, but there's certainly love there—even if they bicker *all the time*.

This chapter will delve into sibling relationships and how they can be a means of support for your child with autism. With everyone cheering your autistic child on, there's no doubt that the family bond will become stronger, and the entire household will embrace the unique dynamics that accompany autism spectrum disorder.

Practical Tips to Strengthen Siblings and Family Bonds

A healthy family dynamic includes a positive relationship between siblings. However, these bonds aren't made as soon as your children are born, but rather something they must forge for themselves. But that doesn't mean that you, the parent, can't help to strengthen the bond among your children as well as the entire family unit.

In this section, we will go over some helpful tips that will not only foster the bond between each individual family member but also create a positive and healthy home environment. Let's dive in, shall we?

Spend Time Together

Think of your family as a team, and for a team to connect and forge a bond, the teammates have to spend quality time together. They need to learn about each other, find out their interests, and communicate effectively. This time together also builds trust, which is the foundation of any type of relationship.

When it comes to spending time together, it doesn't really matter what you do, as long as the time is spent together. You could watch a family favorite movie, have a bonfire, cook s'mores, or even play a fun board game. If you have teenagers in the home, they might find a game of charades to be "boring" or "lame," but once the laughing starts, they will be happy that they decided to participate. Of course, you don't have to do this every single night, but at least pick one night a week when everyone puts their phones down and laptops away, making this particular night a distraction-free family night.

Plan Vacations and Outings

When your child is first diagnosed with autism, the idea of vacations and family outings went right out the window. Between a disruption in their routine, being far from home, the travel time, and new sights and sounds, it probably sounded more like a nightmare than an opportunity to have a good time. However, it doesn't have to be that way.

If your family plans to go on vacation or an outing, you can prepare your child for what's to come. Surely, you want everyone to have a good time, so it's best to get your autistic child ready for what's to come once you figure out the destination. Spend time showing your child YouTube videos of all the cool things they can participate in to get them excited and work on issues they may be struggling with, such as eating at restaurants.

Also, try not to make every outing about your autistic child. Attempt to find activities everyone shows interest in, or maybe just one of your other children. This can give you the opportunity to spend quality time with your children individually and give them the attention they deserve. Nothing is wrong with spending time with one child, doing something they like, while the other parent participates in an activity one of the other children prefers. It just gives you something to talk about over dinner, which is the next topic!

Talk to Each Other

Effective communication is paramount for any relationship, especially when trying to strengthen the family bond. It's crucial to take time out of your day to talk, preferably when distractions aren't around. Talk about each other's day, what your children learned at school, something interesting you saw or heard—pretty much anything you can think of. The point is, just talk to one another.

Having a friendly conversation over dinner is great, but don't forget about the occasional private, heart-to-hearts that come with being a parent. If you notice that one of your children is having a hard time, pull them aside and talk to them about what's going on in private. Listen to them as they discuss their feelings, validate their emotions, and encourage your children to do the same for their siblings. Although parents like to believe that their kids can talk to them about anything, sometimes the topic is something only a sibling can help with.

Build a Healthy Atmosphere

Every parent and child wants to live in a healthy environment, surrounded by the people they love. However, every home has a different idea of what a happy, healthy family consists of. There are many different types of parenting types, each with its own pros and cons, but they all have one thing in common: consistency. I know by now you are probably tired of hearing that word, but there's a good reason why I keep mentioning it.

Consistency provides you and your children with a sense of security. Everyone knows what to expect, thus cutting down on feelings of tension, stress, and anxiety. This predictability also applies to every aspect, from schedules to discipline to parenting style, meaning you can't be authoritative one day and lenient the next.

Treat all Children Equally

While I understand that much of your attention is given to your neurodivergent child, as therapy sessions and meltdowns can become quite frequent. However, you must extend your focus to all of your other children. In Chapter 4, you read how many siblings can have negative feelings toward their autistic sibling, whether it's displayed as jealousy, resentment, overprotectiveness, or completely withdrawing from the family.

Although I'm sure you have come to realize the importance of focusing on each of your children individually by now, you should also discipline all of your children the same way. When your neurodivergent child intentionally misbehaves, don't just brush it off and excuse their behavior because "they have a condition" or "don't know any better." This can cause your other children to feel resentment toward their autistic sibling.

Educate Other Siblings About Autism

Knowing that your sibling has autism and actually understanding the aspects of the disorder are two different things. This might be a little difficult if the sibling is younger, so be sure to use age-appropriate language. For example, you could tell them that their sibling with autism acts differently than them because they have a condition that makes it difficult for them to communicate with others, understand directions, and play a certain way. Tell them that just because their sibling does or acts differently, they are still amazing at other things, like drawing, figuring out math problems, or writing awesome stories.

As for older children and teenagers, you can explain it the same way but contain more facts. They may be embarrassed by how their sibling sometimes acts, especially if a meltdown occurs in public, but you can explain that these reactions often come with the disorder. Their sibling isn't doing it intentionally to embarrass them but rather because their autistic sibling feels overwhelmed by emotions, stimuli, large crowds, or a combination of the three. Having both neurodivergent and neurotypical children can have its own set of challenges, but by educating them about autism, you are defeating ignorance and stigma with actual facts. Not only will this help your child's siblings understand them better, but it will also teach them about diversity and kindness toward others.

Conclusion

As you can see, it's possible to build a strong bond between your autistic child and their siblings. Essentially, it all boils down to a few things:

- **Effective communication:** Being open and honest with your neurotypical children about autism and what the condition entails is the best way for them to be educated. Of course, make sure your explanation is appropriate for the child's age so they can accurately understand.

- **Don't play favorites:** As discussed in Chapter 4, siblings can become overwhelmingly jealous or even depressed when their parents focus all of their attention on the child with autism. They crave your attention as well and can feel neglected if they feel as if they aren't given the attention they deserve. The same sentiment applies to discipline.

- **Building a cohesive family unit:** Once everyone is on the same page, it's much easier for your children to feel secure in their relationship with you and their role within the family. It also provides a sense of consistency and predictability to their day, which every child benefits from.

The truth is, we all want our family to be happy. We want our connection with our spouse and children to stay strong for the rest of our lives. However, to have that, we have to work at these relationships for them to be happy and healthy. We also have to prepare our family for the future, which is the subject of our next chapter.

CHAPTER 11

Preparing for the Future

The way we look at our children and their limitations is precisely the way they will feel about themselves. We set the examples, and they learn by taking our cue from us.

Amalia Starr

Dreaming about your children's future can be terrifying at best, especially if they aren't as independent as you hope they would be. You find yourself wondering how they would ever be able to live by themselves when they struggle to make a grilled cheese on their own without almost burning the house down. Or possibly even questioning how they will be able to handle their future college workload after they had forgotten their math book in their locker for the third time this month. How can you be so sure they could make it out there, in the big world, all on their own without your guidance?

That's why, in this chapter, we will discuss the unique challenges and considerations that come into play when a child with autism is transitioning into adulthood. We will take an in-depth look at topics such as employment, independent living, and accessing various adult services.

Role of Parents and Caregivers in the Transition Phase

Preparing your child for the future is heartbreaking, to say the least. You spend years teaching them to be independent and self-sufficient just so you can say goodbye as they move out and on with their lives. However, when you have a child with autism, this big transition and life change takes more work, effort, patience, and motivation for both you and your child.

According to Dr. Kristin Sohl, a Child's Health professor and founder of ECHO Autism, you should start thinking about what the future will look like for your child when they're around 12 years old or start puberty (2022). When hormones start to run rampant, and their bodies begin to change as they transition into adulthood, or young adulthood in their case, other things begin to change as well. Everything from treatment to school to even friends and responsibilities begins to change, and you want to make sure they're ready for what's to come. The most important change that needs to happen around this age is the life skills they will need to become more independent. So, how do you make this transition run smoother? Let's find out!

Explore and Plan the Necessary Steps in the Transition

As you just read, you should start thinking about your child's future when they start puberty. Take time to talk with your child and ask what they see themselves doing 10, 15, or 20 years from now. Find out what career field they are interested in and how they plan to pursue their goal. For example, if they would like to become a nurse, what type of nurse would they like to be? Do they want to work with children, individuals with special needs, or senior citizens? What inspired them to choose this field of work and which of their strengths would help them with this endeavor? What life skills, or skills in general, will they need to work on to become a nurse?

Once you and your child have had this discussion, the two of you, as a team, can start doing research. Find programs they can enroll in to explore this career field and grow the skills they will need. Even if they are a little too young right now to join a vocational program, I'm sure there are skills they will need that the two of you can work on at home. If you need some advice or guidance on what else your child should work on, you could ask their school counselor or occupational therapist. They can point both of you in the right direction. But, the good news is, if your child is between the ages of 16–18 and has an IEP, their school system can help refer them to adult services, which focuses on helping adults with special needs develop their life skills as they transition into adulthood.

Focus on Vocational and Life Skill Training

It's important to remember that not every child is interested in going to college, and that's okay. Secondary education isn't for everybody, but they should at least have some idea about what they would like to do after graduating high school, and this is where vocational and life skill training comes in.

Unfortunately, life skills aren't likely to be discussed during an IEP meeting, meaning that this is a skill that you, along with your child's network of doctors and therapists, will have to take on without the school's help. However, this doesn't mean that you are completely alone. Do your research and I'm sure you will be able to find programs in your area that help teens with autism, intellectual disabilities, or other conditions such as Down's Syndrome. These programs hold classes to help teach your child how to cook, balance a checkbook, and fill out job applications. Some even teach them how to prepare for a job interview.

Create Long-Term Plans

From living arrangements to how they intend to take care of themselves, the transition to independence is a big one. And this substantial change is one that needs an achievable and realistic plan. When it comes to living on their own, you could always discuss this topic with adult services. Many of these programs help arrange housing for individuals with special needs and will help make accommodations if needed. They can also help set them up with a job so they can pay the bills.

Once you have compiled this crucial information, you and your child can sit down and discuss their options. Ask them whether they plan to use adult services to get their own apartment, whether they would prefer to enroll in college or a vocational program, and then their goal for the future. Once all this has been discussed, it's time to write it all down. Take their goal and break it down into steps, such as learning certain skills like cooking, communicating, or anything they may be behind on but will need to achieve in order to fulfill their goal. Then, when they have strengthened this skill, praise their efforts and move on to the next goal.

Map Out Strategies to Help Your Child Become Independent

Once you have helped your child develop their long-term plan, it's time for you to figure out where and when you will be needed to assist them. For example, if your child would like to enroll in classes that focus on the culinary arts but struggle to make toast, you could foster their interest by developing a strategy where they help you cook dinner every night. Not only will this encourage them to build on their self-sufficiency skills, but it will also give them an idea of whether this career field is something they want to pursue. The point is that you are your child's biggest support system, and by figuring out what strategies will help them to become more independent, you are teaching them valuable skills while encouraging them to keep going.

Assist Your Child in Developing Their Ideas While Fostering Their Interests

If your child doesn't know what they would like to pursue once they have that high school diploma in their hand, they can always consider what topics they have a strong interest in. They can then find a vocational school that teaches this subject or similar topics, and they can learn more about it. This training will not only foster their interest, but also prepare them for what they will find in the career field. Take it from Dr. Temple Grandin, who is on the autism spectrum herself, as she once told a journalist, Scott Barry Kaufman (2013), "Obsessions, when properly directed, can lead some children into a successful career."

Prepare Your Child to Embrace Change

If you begin preparing your child for the future early on, you have much more time to work on skills they will benefit from when they are on their own. Teach them about the importance of organization and time management, as many employers find these particular skills crucial in the work environment. Also, try to talk about the future often and their feelings about change. If they are scared about what's to come, allow them to tell you *why* they're afraid to live on their own or go to college. You can then take those fears and work on them one by one until they become more comfortable with the subject.

Remember, everyone is afraid of change, and it's okay to tell your child that so they don't feel as though they are the only person in the world to deal with these uncertainties. Change is uncomfortable, but it is a necessary evil so we don't become stagnant. The best thing to do is embrace it, as it often leads to bigger and better things.

Provide Motivational Support to Your Child

You have, without a doubt, always been your child's biggest cheerleader. You and your significant other have pushed them to keep going, even if you had to help them up and brush them off after they fail. When planning for their future, your child needs you, now more than ever, to continue your motivational efforts. They need to see that you believe in them, just like you have in the past when they doubted themselves.

Of course, you don't have to throw a huge party after they have championed a skill they have struggled with. Sometimes, a simple "I'm so proud of you" will do. When they struggle to figure something out, encourage them to keep trying and never give up. Many of the life skills that adults need to know to be independent are hard for many teenagers, neurodivergent or not. So, if they feel like giving up, remind them of their goals and encourage them to keep going.

Conclusion

Your nights might be wracked with worry, wondering how your child will ever make it in this world without you. However, I assure you that it's possible. Many individuals with autism are thriving, some of them even becoming doctors, nurses, actors, engineers, and computer techs. Your child can be one of the many great people on Earth who proves nay-sayers wrong, showing them that someone with autism is just as capable, if not more, of living a fulfilling life.

In our next chapter, you will see how families like yours can be an inspiration for parents of a newly diagnosed child. You will read stories that fill your heart with happiness and hope and remind you that a neurological disorder doesn't mean your child can't have it all. So, if you're ready to finish this book with a smile on your face, and possibly tears in your eyes, move on to the next chapter.

CHAPTER 12

Stories of Triumph Inspiring Journeys

It takes a village to raise a child. It takes a child with autism to raise the consciousness of the village.

Coach Elaine Hall

If you have friends within the autism community, you have probably realized how different their family dynamics are compared to yours or your other friends. While some may just be started on this journey, some might be vets with all the advice in the world. Nevertheless, they have all struggled at some point, whether it's during the diagnosis process or trying to help their child strengthen the skills they are lacking. You, yourself, might find common ground within their struggles and feel as though things will never get better.

Well, that's the very reason why I included this chapter. I wanted to show that this journey isn't all winding paths and dark forests. There is a rainbow at the end, and the pot of gold you are searching for is a happy, thriving child.

In this chapter, I will be gifting you five inspirational stories of different families who made a positive change in the lives of their autistic children. They did so by covering the long distance from tackling various challenges to achieving ultimate victory over ASD. I hope these stories will help pull you out of the dark space you have found yourself in and look forward to the future.

Jennifer and Kinley Cuberson

Although I don't particularly like to remember the events that unfolded due to COVID-19, as I feel we all try to forget the time we were stuck in quarantine, we must accept that it happened and turned the lives of many families upside down. Our first story proves that a disruption in a child with autism's schedule can make life a little harder for everyone involved.

Jennifer Cuberson is a stay-at-home mom to nine-year-old Kinley, as well as her four-year-old son and 18-month-old twins. You can probably imagine that Jennifer already had her hands full before everyone was advised to stay at home due to the coronavirus. Before life went into lockdown, Kinley was meeting with a psychologist on a regular basis, consistently seeing her doctor every two weeks as she worked on her communication and socialization skills. However, COVID brought the Cuberson family's predictable schedule to an abrupt end.

All hope was not lost, though, as Jennifer states that Kinley's psychologist was a lifesaver when dealing with the pandemic. The psychologist moved her meetings with the nine-year-old from in-person to virtual and even started sending the young girl information on the virus and tips on how she could keep working on the communication skills they had been working on while she was stuck at home. Kinley's psychologist also started utilizing a reward system for the young girl, encouraging her to keep practicing everything she had learned.

The lockdown wasn't the only thing that changed for Kinley either. In fact, once the quarantine had been lifted, Jennifer and her husband decided to unenroll Kinley from in-person school and start virtual learning. Although it was hard for Kinley at first, Jennifer is happy to say that her daughter is thriving in online school, and her grades are the highest they have ever been.

Mark and Matthew Naughton

Dedicated to his life as a parent of an autistic child, Mark Naughton has used his experiences with his son, Matthew, to encourage other parents that better days are coming. Working as a Senior Business Analyst at the company TalkTalk, Mark also founded his own company, TalkNeurodiversity. In a 2021 article for the blog Ambitious About Autism, Mark shared his and Matthew's story.

Mark's experience with autism began when his child was 15 months old, as he stated that Matthew seemed completely normal for the first year of his life. However, as his son approached his second birthday, Mark and his wife realized that the toddler wasn't speaking. Instead, Matthew would just make sounds in order to communicate with those around him. He also preferred to play with his parents rather than children his own age, would line up toys in an organized manner, and his behavior had become difficult to handle.

Matthew started speech therapy around age two to help with his communication struggles. Mark's wife, who had worked in speech therapy before their son was born, knew what the young boy's communication delay could possibly mean. Unfortunately, suspecting your child might be autistic and receiving an actual diagnosis are two different things. Matthew didn't receive an official diagnosis for another year and a half after starting speech therapy.

Although autism was suspected, Mark and his wife were still shocked to hear their son really was on the spectrum. However, once the shock wore off, they jumped into action. Mark's wife quit the job she had held for a decade and became a stay-at-home mom so she could place all of her focus on Matthew and his needs. Mark, who had been a constable on the police force for 20 years, also left his job to guide his son through life using the strategies Matthew had learned from early intervention therapies.

Matthew's skills in speech and communication grew, and before he knew it, Mark was sending his son off to school. At first, the new kindergartener was enrolled in a school that primarily taught children on the spectrum. There, Matthew received help from his amazing teacher, Rosemary. The teacher helped guide the young boy and even assisted in Mathew receiving an ADHD diagnosis, which allowed him to start medication management in order to help him focus.

Once it was time to begin high school, Mark and his wife decided that Matthew was ready for a new transition: mainstream schooling. During his time there, the teen thrived in his classes. However, Mark attributes his son's success to the IEP provision that was utilized so Matthew could get the help he needed.

At the time of the article, two years ago, Matthew was getting ready to start college with the dream of working on computers. Mark also proudly states that his son's level of confidence and independence has grown exponentially due to the help he received in school. Now, if that's not an inspiring success story, I don't know what is.

Cheryl and Braylen Clayton

According to his mother, Braylen was always a quiet baby. People would actually praise Cheryl for her son's quality, telling her he must be a very good boy. However, that silence began to worry her when his first birthday came and went, and he had yet to start talking or even responding to his name.

To calm her worries, Cheryl and her husband, Mike, took Braylen to an audiologist for a hearing test. Their thoughts were that maybe Braylen's ability to hear was affecting his speech or ability to respond when they called for him. However, the hearing test came back and Braylen's hearing was fine. Unfortunately, this wasn't the news that Cheryl wanted to hear.

Cheryl was a school teacher, and the possibility of her son being on the autism spectrum was likely. This she knew for sure, but she had wished that her son's hearing was to blame. Luckily, the audiologist who had completed the hearing test on Braylen recommended that the toddler start early intervention therapy, as he suspected that something else was going on with the child. Through a state-sponsored program, the toddler was given a full evaluation by a behavioral and developmental pediatrician, where they eventually received the answer Cheryl already knew was coming: Braylen had autism.

Braylen's early intervention included speech and occupational therapy. He was also enrolled in special education classes and joined a weekly playgroup for children on the spectrum. Over time, Cheryl and Mike watched their son proudly as his communication, speech, and socialization skills grew.

Braylen's mother states that while, yes, the progress the child made was slow and steady, the help he received through school, therapy, and the strategies she and Mike continued to work on with Braylen at home definitely contributed to his growth. When Cheryl's story was published by The Children's Hospital of Philadelphia's website in 2016, she happily reported that the seven-year-old was excelling in school, especially when it came to writing and math. He still uses the techniques he learned in occupational therapy, and she contributes much of his progress to the wonderful team of experts and teachers who have been there to support her son and family as a whole.

Niall and Ellison MacMillan

Despite Niall's days being filled with producing content for social media, he is also a father of three, with one of his children being on the autism spectrum. Ellison is the youngest of the three children in the MacMillan home, and his father has made it his sole mission in life to educate parents of autistic children about the realities of the disorder through the experiences he has had with his son.

Like many parents, Niall started something with Ellison was amiss during the COVID-19 lockdown. Since he already had two children, he knew what to expect, but it had appeared as if someone had pressed the pause button on Ellison's development. What were once attempts to talk and communicate, even babbling, had suddenly stopped completely.

Initially, Niall brushed off this disruption in Ellison's milestones, blaming it on his being a "quarantine baby." However, his wife wouldn't let that excuse slide, and she continued to push further as she searched for a legitimate answer. Thanks to her due diligence, Niall's wife was able to have Ellison evaluated and discovered that the couple's son was autistic.

When Niall's article was published on the National Autistic Society's website (n.d.), he reported that Ellison was getting ready to start kindergarten. Although the teachers and specialists have helped the four-year-old to progress in communication and socializing, he still struggles with other issues attributed to autism. For example, Ellison still struggles with transitions and has the occasional meltdown when plans change unexpectedly. He also struggles when staying away from his parents overnight or visiting a crowded place. Even so, both of his parents are extremely proud of how far he has come and hope that Niall's documentation of Ellison's progress on social media helps others to become more accepting of those with autism.

Erin and Izabelle Leach

Izabelle came into this world a month early, but she was by no means what one would expect a premature baby to look like. She weighed almost seven pounds and was extremely healthy despite the unexpected early birth. As she got older, Erin states that Izabelle was very quick to learn new things and was even talking in full sentences before she was a year old.

Being the second child of the family, she picked up things very quickly after spending time with her older sister. Then, shortly after she turned two and her younger sister was born, Izabelle started to behave strangely. While she was still ahead of her developmental milestones, she became extremely aggressive. She would kick, bite, and even stab the members of her family with forks or whatever sharp object she could find. Plus, she was hyperactive and couldn't sit still for longer than a minute, often running around the table as she ate.

By the age of three, she had managed to get three different babysitters to quit due to her misbehavior, all within a matter of months. This made it difficult for her mother to work or keep a job, as she often had to leave the office to pick up her children. Then, sensory issues began to creep up, and Izabelle would fight Erin when it came to wearing certain fabrics, eating particular foods due to texture, and even fighting her parents when it came to taking a bath due to the water being too hot—despite that the water was often nearly freezing.

As time went on, Izabelle's behavior only got worse, as did her sensory issues. Her parents accommodated her needs, but knew something was going on with her that they weren't seeing. Finally, after being referred to a neurologist by her pediatrician, Izabelle then received a referral to be evaluated by a psychologist. Unfortunately, they didn't receive the results they, or Izabelle's neurologist and behavioral therapist, thought they would get. The psychologist stated that Izabelle was anxious, and she did not have ASD or ADHD (although she had already been diagnosed with the latter).

Luckily, Erin didn't stop when it came to advocating for her daughter, nor did Izabelle's neurologist. Her doctor told the girl's mother to get a second opinion, as he was 100% certain that she was on the spectrum—he just couldn't diagnose her himself. Erin's advocacy didn't stop there either, as she continued to accommodate her child's needs and made sure that all of Izabelle's teachers knew what was happening.

Today, Izabelle is in middle school, and although she's on the waiting list to be re-evaluated, she is thriving in a technology and engineering-focused magnet school where many students are on the spectrum. The 13-year-old also knows that there's a high likelihood that she is autistic and embraces her uniqueness. She states that she loves to spend her time drawing anime cartoons and has even sold her artwork to some of her friends.

Before we move onto the departing words of this book, I want to point out the key themes of the inspiring stories you just read:

- Consistency is key and will make a big difference in your child's ability to learn.

- A strong support system can make the impossible become reality.

- Early intervention therapies and strategies can be a god-send when it comes to autism treatment.

- Although I know you want to, you can't do everything for your child. There are going to be good days and bad; just try to stay patient as you navigate toward their future.

- Your child is their own person and will progress at their own pace. You should have to be there to encourage them and cheer them on.

Conclusion

I know of nobody who is purely autistic or purely neu-rotypical. Even God had some autistic moments, which is why the planets all spin.

Jerry Newport

As we prepare to bid each other adieu, I want to reiterate the most important aspect of autism: it truly is a spectrum. No two children with the condition are alike, nor will they exhibit their symptoms in the same exact way. While some may be nonverbal, others might be hyperactive and have sensory issues. Either way, all that matters is that you are there for them, support them, and love them unconditionally as they make their way through this crazy thing we call life.

Also, if you haven't noticed, there is a prominent theme that has been presented throughout each and every chapter. That theme would be the importance of a strong support system. This is crucial not just for your child but also for you—the parent. Both of you need a compassionate community of friends, family, and medical professionals to encourage you, ease your stress, and push you forward when your day-to-day life feels as if it's too much to handle. Utilize these unsung heroes, as they might be the light at the end of the autism tunnel, guiding you toward you and your child's bright future. That's also why I wrote this book: to help guide you through the symptoms, diagnosis, and everything afterward.

So, when you feel you don't know where to turn or just want to refresh your memory on the information you read within these pages, you know this book is here for you and your family. In Chapter 1, we discussed the six Ws of autism, answering what autism is, the age at which most children are diagnosed, what autism looks like for both the child and the parent, why boys are diagnosed more often than girls, and what statistics have to say about children with this disorder. We also demystified some of the most common fallacies surrounding autism spectrum disorder.

In Chapter 2, we discussed the risk factors of autism, along with the early signs and symptoms. We also discussed what to do if you notice these signs in your child, the screening process, and which type of medical professionals you can turn to for answers. Meanwhile, in Chapter 3, you learned about the various health conditions that are commonly associated with ASD, such as ADHD, anxiety, and intellectual disorders, and the reason why your child might be having a hard time sleeping at night.

In Chapter 4, we dove into the early challenges that children with autism face, like dealing with a jealous sibling, an unhealthy home environment, the importance of a consistent schedule, and more common medical conditions often linked with ASD. We also discussed the importance of building a strong support system and how it can help everyone within the family home. Then, in Chapter 5, we spoke strategy. We went over why it's important to nurture your child as they grow, as this form of support helps your child to build strong relationships with others, develops their confidence and sense of resilience, and fosters their learning potential.

Then, we moved on to Chapter 6, where we discussed the many strengths that a child with autism can have, including having an exceptional memory, an eye for detail, and an unparalleled creative side. Not to mention an autistic child's amazing and unique way of thinking, especially when it comes to problem-solving. Chapter 7 was about how to help our child navigate their way through the school system and receive the support they deserve through an IEP.

Chapter 8 was a big one, as it's often what makes parents worry the most: dealing with changes and transitions. Hopefully, reading about why change is difficult for a child with autism and how to make transitions easier for them will help you sleep better at night. The next chapter, Chapter 9, was all about parents and the many ways they can manage their stress, one feeling we often experience as a parent with a neurodivergent child.

In Chapter 10, we discussed family dynamics and how to strengthen the bond within the family home. I even included some practical tips to help you along the way. Then, in Chapter 11, we dove deeper into what to expect as you help your child plan for the future and learned what your role as the parent is as your child transitions into an independent adult.

Last but not least, Chapter 12 gifted you with some amazing stories of triumph, all surrounding children with autism and their families. It's my hope that these stories enlightened you and made you look forward to what's to come. Also, I wanted you to see that even though life might seem difficult right now, it does get better with time and the right amount of support.

Now that you are here, though, in the last few pages of this long journey, I would like to take this time to not only acknowledge but also appreciate your efforts. I know some days are hard for you right now, but you keep pushing forward and are committed to helping your child thrive in this world. And, although our time together is coming to an end, I want to leave you with a few questions to ponder. How have your views on autism changed since reading this book? How can you overcome the negative impact and stigma that autism has had on you and your child? Lastly, how do you envision your child's future?

If this book has impacted how you view autism spectrum disorder and has helped you make it through your toughest times, I would appreciate it if you left a review so other parents, teachers, and possibly even doctors know that this book can help them as well.

Chapter "Good Will"

Helping others without expectation of anything in return has been proven to lead to increased happiness and satisfaction in life.

I would love to give you the chance to experience that same feeling during your reading or listening experience today...

All it takes is a few moments of your time to answer one simple question:

Would you make a difference in the life of someone you've never met—without spending any money or seeking recognition for your good will?

If so, I have a small request for you.

If you've found value in your reading experience today, I humbly ask that you take a brief moment right now to leave an honest review of this book. It won't cost you anything but 30 seconds of your time—just a few seconds to share your thoughts with others.

Your voice can go a long way in helping someone else find the same inspiration and knowledge that you have.

Are you familiar with leaving a review for a Kindle, or e-reader book? If so, it's simple:

If you're reading on **Kindle** or an e-reader, simply scroll to the last page of the book and swipe up—the review should prompt from there. Or you can follow those direct links **Amazon USA** / **Amazon UK** which will take you directly to the review page.

If you're on a **Paperback** or any other physical format of this book, you can find the book page on Amazon (or wherever you bought this) and leave your review right there. Scan the barcode to be taken to the review page on Amazon:

Amazon US Review

Amazon UK Review

About Natalie Loveson

Natalie Loveson's journey into autism advocacy began when her son was diagnosed with Autism Spectrum Disorder at age two. As a nurse with a background in biomedical research, she approached this new chapter with both professional curiosity and maternal determination.

The turning point came when she realized that textbook knowledge wasn't enough. Through daily experiences with her son, she learned to see the world through his unique perspective. This blend of professional insight and personal experience shaped her approach to autism parenting.

Today, Natalie shares her knowledge through her books and blog, offering practical strategies that work in real-world situations. Her writing comes from a place of genuine understanding - she's lived through the challenges, celebrated the victories, and learned that every autistic child has their own path to success.

Drawing from her healthcare background and years of hands-on parenting experience, she provides other families with the tools and insights she wishes she'd had at the start of her journey. Her message is simple: with understanding, support, and the right strategies, every autistic child can thrive in their own unique way.

To follow her work, visit Ausome Parenting Books website (https://ausomeparentingbooks.com/) or follow her on Amazon, BookBub or Goodreads.

Amazon Author Follow

BookBub Author Follow

GoodReads Author Follow

Also By Natalie Loveson

In **"Ausome Connections"** Natalie Loveson offers practical strategies to build your autistic child social confidence and navigate challenges. This guide provides tools for understanding friendship rules, handling teasing, promoting inclusion approach and much more to boost social skills.

"Ausome Journey" offers the essential tools and insights you need to understand your autistic child and advocate for their needs. Drawing on both medical expertise and real-life experience, this guide helps you navigate education, communication, safety, and community engagement.

References

ACES. (2022, April 15). *Stages of acceptance of your child's autism diagnosis*. ACESABA. https://www.acesaba.com/aba/stages-of-acceptance

Ankrom, S. (2021, March 20). *How to breathe properly for relieving your anxiety*. Verywell Mind. https://www.verywellmind.com/abdominal-breathing-2584115

Arky, B. (2023, June 16). *Why many autistic girls are overlooked*. Child Mind Institute. https://childmind.org/article/autistic-girls-overlooked-undiagnosed-autism/#:~:text=More%20boys%20are%20diagnosed%20with

AUTISM AND DEVELOPMENTAL DISABILITIES MONITORING (ADDM) NETWORK. (n.d.

) (2023) https://www.cdc.gov/ncbddd/autism/pdf/ADDM-Community-Report-SY2020-h.pdf

Autism Speaks. (n.d.). *Medical conditions associated with autism.* Autism Speaks. https://www.autismspeaks.org/medical-conditions-associated-autism#adhd

Autism Speaks. (2021). *What is autism?* Autism Speaks. https://www.autismspeaks.org/what-autism

Autism Speaks. (2023, March 23). *Autism speaks pledges to make world of difference as autism prevalence rises to 2.7% of children in U.S.* Autism Speaks. https://www.autismspeaks.org/press-release/autism-speaks-pledges-make-world-difference-autism-prevalence-rises-27-children-us

Autism Specialty Group. (2021, December 24). *Importance of consistency in autism, routine and autism.* Autism Specialty Group. https://www.autismspecialtygroup.com/blog/importance-of-consistency-in-autism

Autism Therapy Group. (2021, March 7). *Caregiver burnout.* Autism Therapy Group. https://atgtogether.com/caring-for-the-caregiver-how-to-avoid-caregiver-burnout

Bahri, N., Sterrett, K., & Lord, C. (2022). Risk factors and pivotal periods: Marital status over 28 years for parents of individuals with autism. *MedRxiv (Cold Spring Harbor Laboratory).* https://www.medrxiv.org/content/10.1101/2022.02.28.22271595v1

Bidhuri, A. (2023, April 2). *Autism awareness day: 10 common myths about autism spectrum disorder*. Healthshots. https://www.healthshots.com/preventive-care/self-care/world-autism-day-stop-believing-these-common-myths-about-autism/#:~:text=Myth%201%3A%20Autism%20is%20a

Brosnan, M., Lewton, M., & Ashwin, C. (2016). Reasoning on the autism spectrum: A dual process theory account. *Journal of Autism and Developmental Disorders, 46*(6), 2115–2125. https://doi.org/10.1007/s10803-016-2742-4

CDC. (2021, December 21). *Vaccines do not cause autism concerns*. Centers for Disease Control and Prevention. https://www.cdc.gov/vaccinesafety/concerns/autism.html

CDC. (2022, December 9). *What is autism spectrum disorder?* Centers for Disease Control and Prevention. https://www.cdc.gov/ncbddd/autism/facts.html

Cibralic, S., Kohlhoff, J., Wallace, N., McMahon, C., & Eapen, V. (2019). A systematic review of emotion regulation in children with Autism Spectrum Disorder. *Research in Autism Spectrum Disorders, 68*. https://doi.org/10.1016/j.rasd.2019.101422

Crespi, B. J. (2016). Autism as a disorder of high intelligence. *Frontiers in Neuroscience, 10*(300). https://doi.org/10.3389/fnins.2016.00300

Crum, A., & Crum, T. (2015, September 3). *Stress can be a good thing if you know how to use it*. Harvard Business Review.

https://hbr.org/2015/09/stress-can-be-a-good-thing-if-you-kno w-how-to-use-it#:~:text=Although%20the%20stress%20response %20can

Dalien, S. (2014, October 15). *5 tips parents can use to help create an effective IEP*. Special Ed Resource. https://specialedresource. com/5-tips-parents-can-use-help-create-effective-iep

Edelson, S. M. (2019, May 6). *Toe walking and ASD*. Autism Research Institute. https://autism.org/toe-walking-and-asd

Elkins, K., & Sharon, A. (2014). *Autism risk factors: Genetics and environment*. Healthline. https://www.healthline.com/health/a utism-risk-factors

FCA. (n.d.). *Benefits of pets for autistic children*. Fostering Autistic Children. https://www.thefca.co.uk/fostering-autistic-children/pets-for-au tistic-children/#:~:text=Helping%20to%20reduce%20stress%20a nd

Gendel, M. (2022, June 27). *Autism signs in infants*. Lighthouse Autism Center. https://lighthouseautismcenter.com/blog/top-s igns-your-infant-may-have-autism

Gold Buscho, A. (2023, February 28). *Divorce and special needs children*. Psychology Today. https://www.psychologytoday.com/intl/blog/a-better-divorce/2 02302/divorce-and-special-needs-children#:~:text=When%20you %20have%20a%20child

Goode, H., & Shinkle, E. (2021, August 25). *3 key takeaways from the strong link between autism & creativity*. Global Teletherapy. https://globalteletherapy.com/3-key-takeaways-autism-creativity-connection

Gross, C. (2022, May 31). *Jealousy in siblings of children with autism*. Circle Care Services. https://circlecareservices.com/jealousy-in-siblings-of-children-with-autism

Hatch, C. (2011, October 17). *Autism 5 times more common among low birth weight babies*. Live Science. https://www.livescience.com/16576-autism-birth-weight-babies.html

Healthdirect. (2022, March 4). *Self-talk*. Healthdirect Australia. https://www.healthdirect.gov.au/self-talk#:~:text=If%20you%20mainly%20think%20positively

Hess, P. (2022, January 11). *Adult autism diagnoses don't routinely follow other diagnoses in childhood*. Spectrum. https://www.spectrumnews.org/news/adult-autism-diagnoses-dont-routinely-follow-other-diagnoses-in-childhood/

ICT. (2017, November 14). *How teaching gratitude supports social & emotional development*. Integrated Children's Therapy. https://integratedchildrens.com/teaching-gratitude-supports-social-emotional-development/

Jones, A. (2023, April 25). *Inspirational quotes for autism (ASD Awareness Month)*. Noodle Nook. https://www.noodlenook.net/inspirational-quotes-for-autism/

Kaufman, S. B. (2013, June 26). *Q & A with Temple Grandin on The Autistic Brain*. Scientific American Blog Network. https://blogs.scientificamerican.com/beautiful-minds/q-a-with-temple-grandin-on-the-autistic-brain/

Keller, D., & Honig, A. S. (2004). Maternal and paternal stress in families with school-aged children with disabilities. *American Journal of Orthopsychiatry, 74*(3), 337–348. https://doi.org/10.1037/0002-9432.74.3.337

Kluth, P. (n.d.). *Supporting students with autism: 10 ideas for inclusive classrooms | Reading Rockets*. Reading Rockets. https://www.readingrockets.org/topics/autism-spectrum-disorder/articles/supporting-students-autism-10-ideas-inclusive-classrooms

Lightner, L. (2022, December 6). *10 best visual timers for kids with autism or ADHD*. A Day in Our Shoes. https://adayinourshoes.com/10-free-visual-timers-for-kids-and-autism/

Lovering, N. (2022, May 3). *Autism and logical thinking: What to know*. Psych Central. https://psychcentral.com/autism/why-people-with-autism-are-more-logical#next-steps

MacMillan, N. (n.d.). *"I never really understood what autism was. Now, I'm in this whole new world with a new understanding of words, acronyms and behaviours."* National Autistic Society. Retrieved September 13, 2023, from https://www.autism.org.uk/advice-and-guidance/stories/stories-from-the-spectrum-meet-niall

Martinelli, K. (2021, August 28). *Why do kids have trouble with transitions?* Child Mind Institute. https://childmind.org/article/why-do-kids-have-trouble-with-tra nsitions/#:~:text=Children%20with%20autism%20have%20a

Mathew, N. E., Burton, K. L. O., Schierbeek, A., Črnčec, R., Walter, A., & Eapen, V. (2019). Parenting preschoolers with autism: Socioeconomic influences on wellbeing and sense of competence. *World Journal of Psychiatry*, *9*(2), 30–46. https://doi.org/10.54 98/wjp.v9.i2.30

Mayo Clinic. (2020, April 22). *Meditation: A simple, fast way to reduce stress.* Mayo Clinic. https://www.mayoclinic.org/tests-pr ocedures/meditation/in-depth/meditation/art-20045858

Moorhead, J. (2021, December 16). *"A lot fell into place": the adults who discovered they were autistic – after their child was diagnosed.* The Guardian. https://www.theguardian.com/society/2021/dec /16/adults-discovered-autistic-child-diagnosed-autism

Nationwide Children's Hospital. (n.d.). *Autism parent training services.* Nationwide Children's. https://www.nationwidechildrens.org/specialties/center-for-autis m-spectrum-disorders/parent-training#:~:text=Focuses%20on%2 0preventing%20and%20treating

Naughton, M. (2015, July 13). *Autism - a parent's story.* Ambitious about Autism. https://www.ambitiousaboutautism.org.uk /about-us/media-centre/blog/autism-parent-story

Nicole. (2022, January 10). *Co-occurring conditions and autism.* Autism Research Institute. https://autism.org/comorbidities-of-autism/#:~:text=Children%20with%20autism%20may%20be

NIH. (2021, April 19). *Early intervention for autism.* National Institute of Health. https://www.nichd.nih.gov/health/topics/autism/conditioninfo/treatments/early-intervention

One Central Health. (2020, October 30). *10 myths about autism spectrum disorder.* One Central Health. https://www.onecentralhealth.com.au/autism/10-myths-about-autism

105 favorite quotes about autism and aspergers. (2019, June 9). The Art of Autism. https://the-art-of-autism.com/favorite-quotes-about-autism-and-aspergers/

Paulos, S. (2018, April 2). *Detecting autism in the very young.* Austin Neuropsychology. https://neuroaustin.com/2018/04/02/detecting-autism-in-the-very-young/

PsyPost. (2023, September 13). *A disturbing number of TikTok videos about autism include claims that are "patently false," study finds.* MSN. https://www.msn.com/en-us/health/other/a-disturbing-number-of-tiktok-videos-about-autism-include-claims-that-are-patently-false-study-finds/ar-AA1gEDNd?ocid=msedgntp&cvid=f76a407e26f74005851608b08ebaebcc&ei=15

Raby, M. (2020, December 15). *Five parents of children with autism share stories and insights on life in 2020.* PBS So-

Cal. https://www.pbssocal.org/education/parents/five-parents-c
hildren-autism-share-stories-insights-life-2020

Raising Children. (2017a, June). *Sensory sensitivities: children and
teenagers with autism spectrum disorder*. Raising Children Network. https://raisingchildren.net.au/autism/behaviour/underst
anding-behaviour/sensory-sensitivities-asd

Raising Children. (2017b, August 2). *Social skills for children with autism spectrum disorder*. Raising Children Network. https://raisingchildren.net.au/autism/communicating-rel
ationships/connecting/social-skills-for-children-with-asd

Raising Children. (2022, October 26). *Conditions that can occur
with autism*. Raising Children Network.
https://raisingchildren.net.au/autism/learning-about-autism/ab
out-autism/conditions-that-occur-with-asd#intellectual-disabilit
y-and-developmental-delays-nav-title

Raising Children Network. (2017, August). *Social stories*. Raising
Children Network. https://raisingchildren.net.au/autism/thera
pies-guide/social-stories

Raising Children Network. (2020, November 18). *Building
confidence: autistic children and teenagers*. Raising Children
N e t w o r k .
https://raisingchildren.net.au/autism/behaviour/understanding
-behaviour/building-confidence-asd#:~:text=You%20can%20buil
d%20confidence%20in

Raising Children Network. (2022a, April 28). *Resilience in autistic children and teenagers*. Raising Children Network. https://raisingchildren.net.au/autism/development/social -emotional-development/resilience-autistic-children-teenagers

Raising Children Network. (2022b, May 24). *Video-modelling*. Raising Children Network. https://raisingchildren.net.au/autism/therapies-guide/video-mo delling#:~:text=Does%20video%2Dmodelling%20help%20autisti c

Rapoport, J., Chavez, A., Greenstein, D., Addington, A., & Gog-tay, N. (2009). Autism spectrum disorders and childhood-onset schizophrenia: Clinical and Biological Contributions to a Rela-tion Revisited. *Journal of the American Academy of Child & Adolescent Psychiatry, 48*(1), 10–18. https://doi.org/10.1097/chi.0b 013e31818b1c63

Sarris, M. (2014, April 8). *Coming of age: autism and the transition to adulthood*. Kennedy Krieger Institute. https://www.kennedykrieger.org/stories/interactive-autis m-network-ian/autism-transition-to-adulthood

Sarris, M. (2016, January 27). *"Recovery" by the numbers: How often do children lose an autism diagnosis?* Kennedy Krieger Institute. https://www.kennedykrieger.org/stories/interactive-autism-netw ork-ian/recovery-numbers-how-often-do-children-lose-autism-di agnosis#:~:text=Two%20major%20U.S.%20studies%20have

Sesame Workshop. (2017, March 7). *Teaching kids about autism.* Sesame Workshop. https://sesameworkshop.org/resources/teaching-kids-autism/#:~:text=Explain%20autism%20to%20young%20children.&text=Kids%20who%20have%20never%20met

Signs of autism in babies and toddlers. (n.d.). Autism SA. https://autismsa.org.au/autism-diagnosis/autism-symptoms/signs-of-autism-in-babies

Sohl, K. (2022, March 31). *Helping teens with autism transition to adulthood: Tips for parents & caregivers.* Healthy Children. https://www.healthychildren.org/English/health-issues/conditions/Autism/Pages/helping-teens-on-the-autism-spectrum-transition-to-adulthood-tips-for-parents-&-caregivers.aspx#:~:text=A%20critical%20part%20of%20transitioning

Sona. (2023, June 2). *What happened to Jacob Barnett? Where is Jacob Barnett now? - News.* Fresherslive. https://www.fresherslive.com/latest/articles/what-happened-to-jacob-barnett-where-is-jacob-barnett-now-1000024598

Special Learning. (2021, November 23). *The importance of support groups.* Special Learning. https://special-learning.com/the-importance-of-support-groups/#:~:text=Support%20groups%20can%20be%20a

SSM Health. (n.d.). *Savant syndrome.* SSM Health. https://www.ssmhealth.com/treffert-center/conditions-treatmen

ts/savant-syndrome#:~:text=Approximately%20one%20in%2010
%20persons

Szalavitz, M. (2012, July 10). *What genius and autism have in common.* Time. https://healthland.time.com/2012/07/10/what
-child-prodigies-and-autistic-people-have-in-common

The Children's Hospital of Philadelphia. (2016, August 23). *Autism Spectrum Disorder: Braylen's Story.* Chop. https://www.chop.edu/stories/autism-spectrum-disorder-braylen-s-story

Thinking Autism. (n.d.). *Kylee's autism recovery story.* Thinking Autism Taking Action. https://www.thinkingautism.org.uk/tak
ing-action/testimonials/kaylees-story-of-recovery

University of East Anglia. (2015, August 13). *Research examines relationship between autism and creativity: New research has found that people with high levels of autistic traits are more likely to produce unusually creative ideas.* ScienceDaily. https://www.sciencedaily.com/releases/2015/08/150813222253.htm

UofM. (2017, November 27). *Why autism strikes mostly boys.* University of Minnesota. https://research.umn.edu/inquiry/post/why-autism-strikes-most
ly-boys#:~:text=Certain%20genetic%20variants%20are%20linked

van Steensel, F. J. A., Bögels, S. M., & Perrin, S. (2011). Anxiety disorders in children and adolescents with autistic spectrum disorders: A meta-analysis. *Clinical Child and Family Psychology*

Review, 14(3), 302–317. https://doi.org/10.1007/s10567-011-0097-0

Zauderer, S. (2023, June 29). *5 ways autism can affect learning.* Cross River Therapy. https://www.crossrivertherapy.com/autism/how-autism-affects-learning#:~:text=In%20conclusion%2C%20autism%20can%20have

Zeldovich, L. (2018, May 9). *Cold parenting? Childhood schizophrenia? How the diagnosis of autism has evolved over time.* Science. https://www.science.org/content/article/cold-parenting-childhood-schizophrenia-how-diagnosis-autism-has-evolved-over-time

Zuckerman, C. (2020, April 30). What should I do if I think my child has autism? *The New York Times.* https://www.nytimes.com/2020/04/30/parenting/toddler/autism-early-diagnosis.html

www.ingramcontent.com/pod-product-compliance
Lightning Source LLC
Chambersburg PA
CBHW070517160726
48003CB00004B/1611